Home and Away

ALSO BY RONALD WRIGHT

HISTORY

Stolen Continents:
The "New World" through Indian Eyes

TRAVEL

Cut Stones and Crossroads: A Journey in Peru
On Fiji Islands
Time Among the Maya

HOME AND AWAY

Ronald Wright

Vintage Books

A Division of Random House of Canada

VINTAGE BOOKS CANADA EDITION, 1994

 Published in Canada by Vintage Books, a division of Random House of Canada Limited, Toronto. First published in Canada in 1993 by Alfred A. Knopf Canada, Toronto. Distributed by Random House of Canada Limited, Toronto.

Canadian Cataloguing in Publication Data

Wright, Ronald
Home and away

ISBN 0-394-28065-2

1. Voyages and travels. 2. Wright, Ronald — Journeys.
I. Title.

G465.W75 1994 910.4 C94-931605-9

Pages 239–240 constitute an extension of the copyright page.

Printed and bound in Canada
10 9 8 7 6 5 4 3 2 1
Toronto, New York, London, Sydney, Auckland

To my parents,
Edward and Shirley Wright,
who have put up with the travels and the traveller

Thanks to Jack McIver, Barbara Moon, George Galt, Bart Robinson, and Matthew Church, for sending me away; to Alberto Manguel for being *sui generis*; to Mark Abley for originating the Yukon languages idea; to Johan Reinhard for information on Andean bullfights; to Raymond Haimila for the gift of *Manco*; to Allan Smith for putting me on the kangaroo trail and George Woodcock for reminding me; to Anthony Weller for telling me to write up my freighter memories. Special thanks to Louise Dennys and Gena Gorrell for deft and patient editing of *Home and Away*, and to my wife, Janice Boddy—as always, editor of first resort.

Contents

ONE

The Captain's Santo

AS A BOY of twelve or thirteen, in an English boarding school, I read books about the sea. Some of these were jingoistic Edwardian adventure stuff; others—Percy F. Westerman, B. Traven's *Ghost Ship*, Lowry's *Ultramarine*—told of the lives of merchant seamen, their carousing, their grimy working-class heroism in the rusting, coal-fired death traps of the early twentieth century, where rivets popped, boilers burst, and rudder chains broke in the middle of Force Nine gales. Of course, the language was cleaned up and you were left with little idea that sailors did anything ashore but drink and gamble. But the sea was alive. The sea was the compelling character. It was usually the cold grey North Atlantic, whose sixty-foot waves tossed iron ships like bathtoys.

When not at school, I lived on the East Anglian coast, where the muddy North Sea nibbles at the land. This was a sad, liminal sea, in which the things of man and nature mingled like messy colours in a paintbox. It washed up jellyfish and skate and sometimes the rotten carcass of a seal—things from within itself—and deposited these beside raw sewage from my town. I formed odd theories about sex on the evidence of tampons and rubbers displayed at low tide. Sometimes at high tide on rough winter days I would peer over the concrete bastion that defended the beach huts, locked up for the season with their teapots and earwigs. I watched six-foot waves crash in plumes against the barrier, and they looked fierce enough. I suspected my authors of exaggeration: I could not believe in waves ten times that size.

It was around this time that my parents asked me what I wanted to be when I grew up. I said I thought I might go to sea. And my father said: "Wonderful life, the Navy. Admiral Sir Ronald Wright!" Was he being serious or ironic? It was his enthusiasm I feared, not his sarcasm. For whenever my parents turned an interest of mine into a dream of grandeur, it immediately became unattainable and undesirable. I couldn't see myself as an admiral at all. "Actually," I said, "it was the merchant navy I was thinking of." My parents didn't like the sound of that. Merchant seamen, they warned sternly, were drinkers and gamblers; they stayed away from home for years at a time; their wives left them and their children hardly knew them. It seemed to me that the same might be true of Her Majesty's navy, but I didn't say so. Nor did I say that much of the sea's lure was precisely *because* it was a life for ruffians and misfits.

Throughout the rest of my childhood I never set foot on any ship larger than a car ferry. We owned a small sailing dinghy during my teenaged years, but I lost interest in it when I discovered motorbikes and girls. My father and his friends sailed on weekends around the East Anglian mud flats; I went on "burn-ups" with the Rockers. I became knowledgeable about crankshafts and cylinder heads; I did "the ton" (a hundred miles per hour) on dubious machinery. I forgot the sea.

After three years at university the old question of what to "be" came up again. It wasn't a question I enjoyed. Silly, I thought, how we confuse being and doing. *What do you do?* means *Who are you?* We are branded with ancient castes: Falconer, Fletcher, Wright. Wright was vague; it begged a prefix: *Wheel-? Cart-? Play-?* I was twenty-one, a Cambridge BA and a husband, and I had no idea what to do. The marriage, a year old and already in ruins, was a mistake. The degree was also a mistake—someone else's. I'd wasted my time at Cambridge; my main exertion had been to devise ways of hiding that fact from tutors. That's how I learned to write, but in those days I could never have made a living as a writer. Apart from essay assignments (which often strayed into fiction) I wrote poetry—a non-starter of a career—and everything I sent out came back.

The sea and the Duke of Edinburgh saved me. Now, to this day I've never met the duke, and I'm sure he has no idea what a service he did me. In 1968—the year before I finished university—he had been to Mexico City in connection with the Olympic Games. There he had met someone in the government who thought it would be a good idea for a few British archaeology students to work on a Mexican dig. Youth, international goodwill, and all that. (Only later did I suspect it was a PR job designed by the Mexicans to counter the bad press they got for the Tlatelolco massacre, when police murdered hundreds of student demonstrators on the very spot where the Aztecs had fought to the death centuries before.) I, too, had been in Mexico that year, visiting ruins with the help of a university grant. My degree was in archaeology and I spoke a little Spanish. So in the summer of 1969 a letter arrived from a certain Major Trench, saying that my name had come up as a potential "group leader" for a thing called Project Montezuma. The thought of leading anything terrified me, and I knew that Mexicans weren't fond of Montezuma, whom they considered a fool for welcoming Cortés. They also hated that particular spelling of his name. But I needed a job. And I needed to get away.

Project Montezuma's first meeting was held at Major Trench's London flat. I met the three I was supposed to lead, and all of us were lectured by Sir Justin Glanders, a wattled gentleman in his eighties who seemed to be an intermediary between Trench and the duke.

"I've always believed there's a special bond between young people and young countries," Sir Justin said, beaming at us pedagogically like a large red toad. "You'll be going to a place that nobody's heard of. Backward. No culture or traditions to speak of. Desperately poor…." A coughing fit shattered this train of thought. I was at the age when I thought one should point out other people's mistakes.

"Mexico's poor, yes, but it has one of the fastest-growing economies in the world," I said. "And it's hardly young. It's as old as Egypt or Greece. And they do archaeology precisely because they value their traditions…."

Major Trench offered drinks all round and beckoned me aside to help him. He cornered me in the passage. "Sir Justin Glanders is a cross we have to bear." He pronounced it "craawse" and glared. But I was unabashed. Elders and betters made me nervous, and that made me cocky.

"About Project Montezuma. We ought to change the name."

"How's that?"

"It ought to be Project Cuauhtémoc—the king who fought the Spaniards—he's the real hero. Mexicans regard Montezuma as a sort of pansy mystic who died with a sword up his bum."

"Can't be done. Nobody's heard of this … of this other chap. Certainly not the duke, or he would have thought of it himself."

"But they don't even spell Montezuma's name with an *n*. It should be Mocte…."

"Too late I'm afraid. We've sent our newsletter to the printers."

This was in October. In November, Trench made arrangements for our travel. The four of us—all male—were to be given free passage aboard a Mexican freighter.

The SS *Tampico* did not live up to my idea of what a Mexican freighter should be. For a start she was almost new—a bronze plaque on the bridge announced that she had been built in Brazil in 1965 and weighed 13,000 tons. The grey sides and brown deck were freshly painted, and her radar dish revolved constantly as if to advertise how up to date she was. We boarded in Le Havre on New Year's Day, after crossing the English Channel by a ferry awash with beer and vomit. Some of the beer and vomit was ours. Two of my colleagues were fellow-drinkers: Brendan, a stocky Irishman who had grown up in England (he had nervous hands that shook and fiddled whenever he had to pay for something); and Dominic, a disingenuously vague Eton boy with shrewd eyes in a large head like a pantomime lion's. Matthew, who was gaunt, scholarly, and had the cold blue gaze and infinite patience of a heron, didn't drink. He carried a small notebook in which he recorded the price of everything: *Cheese roll (snack, ferry)—1 shilling and sixpence. Black coffee and croissant (breakfast, Le Havre)—2 francs. Taxi to docks—15 francs.* "I want to know absolutely everything," Major Trench had told him. "The cost of everything. The address of everyone. Who you saw. Who helped you. Who didn't. You're the pioneers. Next time, with your information, we'll know what to do. Got it?" And Matthew, who looked suitably pedantic and reliable, had assumed this task.

"I saw that cheese roll of yours swimming for its life," Brendan said. "Shouldn't you make a note of it? You know—*Snack, lost to seasickness, English Channel.* Old Trench will have to know."

We were given empty cabins on the bridge. Mine had PILOTO written above the door. It was like a railway sleeping car: a single bunk on one side, a desk, a washbasin, and a narrow cupboard. Apart from a red vinyl couch that looked like the front seat of an American car, it was tasteful. The built-in furniture was varnished mahogany, the formica on the walls subdued. The sink had a clean towel and a pink bar of soap with *Camay de México* stamped into its shiny surface. Only the porthole above the desk gave the cabin a nautical air. That and a subtle, unsettling motion, a complex heave and sway, caused by the echo of the sea's movements in the harbour and the loading of freight from dock to hold.

From my porthole I had a view forward, along the deck. The *Tampico* was loading herself by means of booms attached to her thick steel masts, which marched in a row down both sides of the ship, one pair for each hold. Each pair was joined at the top by a steel lintel, which supported a crane operator's cab. The squat masts were architectural, industrial, they made you think of colonnades; they held no suggestion of the days of sail. Beyond them, perhaps a hundred yards from the bridge, rose the triangular beak of the foredeck, inhabited only by giant winches. Evidently, the days of the forecastle—where sailors lived in sea stories—were also gone. Lower ranks merely lived lower down in the bridge, some beneath the water line.

So far we'd met only the steward, a thin, sallow, elderly fellow who had the air of a long-time waiter in a suburban bar. He had shown us to our quarters and told us to appear for breakfast the following morning at seven o'clock. For the rest of the day—New Year's Day—we were on our own, wandering the rainy cobbles of Le Havre, buying postcards and snacks, sipping *café noir* in the one establishment that was open, a grim stone cave decorated with bullfight posters. Our breakfast jollity wore off. We sat quietly, four strangers with little to say. I thought of my parents, my estranged wife, and a student nurse I'd met shortly before Christmas. None of them had seen me off at the station; I hadn't wanted them there. I wanted no one to know I had any ties to another human being. Behind me was a mess; I was running away to sea.

The next morning at breakfast we met some of the officers but saw no sign of the captain. Presiding at the main table was the first mate, a tall, imposing man of fifty with a broad mouth defined by a pencil-thin moustache and trim goatee, like a Maya lord from an ancient vase. He leant back in his chair, fixed you with an even gaze, and spoke Spanish slowly and clearly as if giving elocution lessons. At first I thought this was for our benefit, but later it became clear he always spoke that way; it gave him a magisterial presence you couldn't help but respect. On his left sat the second mate, a Mexican of Japanese descent with a slight frame and a look of frozen disappointment on his boyish face. He was tapping a fried tortilla with his knife, pronouncing it *muy duro*, very hard. Opposite the Japanese sat a short, silent, Aztec-looking fellow with the calm alertness of a cat. He seemed to be listening to the ship, her noises and rhythms, expecting the unexpected. He was the chief engineer.

The steward steered us four gringos to a table of our own beneath a large square porthole. The dining lounge straddled the superstructure below the bridge. Like the cabins it was plain and neat, with an orange felt carpet (a popular style in 1970) and walls of pale formica panelling with mahogany trim. On the starboard side of the room was a door marked CAPITAN. An identical door—open—on the port side led to the owner's suite, which I could see had a double berth and private shower. "The captain uses that when he brings his wife," the first mate volunteered. "But it's empty now. One of you could use it, but you might find it noisy when we have our little parties here." At this the others laughed.

"*¿Qué desean?*" asked the steward impatiently, and we laughed at the literal translation, *What do you desire?*

"How about the captain's wife?" said Brendan in English, grinning at the steward, who shrugged, went away to the galley, and came back with the works. I had forgotten the size of Mexican breakfasts: fried eggs and a bludgeoned leathery steak, a tall stack of tortillas, puddles of sour cream on refried beans. Both steak and eggs were smothered in blistering chile sauce. The sharp chile vapour and the bland steam from the tortillas—an aroma of mortar and corn—took me instantaneously to Mexico.

Freight kept coming aboard all that day and the next. Le Havre rose beside us and I thought about the Plimsoll line: did ships still have them? We took on a few European luxuries—smelly cheeses in crates and Mercedes Benzes smeared with grease to guard their beauty, like night cream on an actress. Most of our cargo was equipment for Mexico City's new underground: running gear for carriages and engines, axles, switches, solid rubber wheels. Loading ceased on the afternoon of our third day in Le Havre; iron lids were winched in sections across the hatches and sealed with tarpaulins. Finally, two huge steel girders—they looked like spans of a bridge and must have weighed scores of tons—were swung aboard by a giant dockside crane and tied down on each side of the deck between hatch and railings. With a lurch to port, then starboard, the *Tampico* stumbled like a mule under their weight.

At about four o'clock, as the drizzle thickened with dusk, the ship began to shudder and twitch like a dog having a bad dream, and coughed a chain of black smoke rings from her funnel. The rhythm of the *Tampico*'s generators, which had become so commonplace I had forgotten it, was upstaged by a gathering convulsion, a *grand mal* building from below. Her engine, I'd already discovered, was no smooth and soulless turbine but a giant diesel with seven pistons the size of wine barrels. The mechanics had been checking this machine in port and had let me enter it by a steel door.

Warped from the dock by a tug, the *Tampico* engaged her screw and steamed into the English Channel. It even felt like steaming. The seizure never ended but as the engine reached working speed it settled into a ponderous syncopation that would rumble the floor, rattle glasses, and blur outlines all the way from France to Mexico.

After two days at sea I agreed with Samuel Johnson: being in a ship is being in jail with the chance of being drowned. It was profoundly boring. There was nothing to do except take a walk along the spray-soaked deck or stand at the taffrail and gaze at the wake fanning across low hills of ocean swell. The churned water was a deep bottle-green, shot with blebs like coarse glass. It exerted the monotonous fascination of an open fire, but its heart was cold and dispiriting, and the air at the stern was often foul with the sulphurous breath of the engines—the reek of a badly ventilated coal furnace.

You had only to turn to the horizon (whenever the line between sea and sky was clear enough to discern) to grasp the enormity of the planet, the great emptiness we were crossing. I realized I would never make a professional sailor. Seasickness wasn't the problem; the problem was claustrophobia. This great circle of grey space might just as well have been a concrete wall; the ship was a floating prison and my sentence would be at least a fortnight. A fortnight doesn't seem very long to me now, but then the days crawled. I couldn't pass much time with books, because to read in a tossing cabin, like reading in a car, *did* make me queasy.

Meals were the main diversion; I looked forward to them as fiercely as a tiger in a zoo. Sometimes the four of us would play cards afterwards—whist, poker, rummy, Black Maria—but as the weather began to worsen the number of players dwindled, and I've never liked cards much anyway. By the fourth day at sea, waves were routinely breaking across the deck. The first mate warned us not to go out any more. Sea doors and portholes were bolted fast. The prison of water shrank to a prison of steel. The bridge began to stink of spilled food, diesel oil, and puke. The steward became more taciturn and impatient than ever, and his trips to the galley were marked by crashing plates and cutlery and lengthy Mexican curses employing the verb *chingar*.

We hadn't seen the captain at all. The door to his cabin was always shut; no sound emerged. Like Ahab, he was never mentioned by the officers. We wondered if he was even aboard. He came out with the storm—it must have been the fifth or sixth day. We were somewhere in the middle of the North Atlantic, in the middle of the northern winter. A gale began to blow. Matthew, the chronicler, hung a ruler from a pin on his cabin wall to measure the ship's roll. He began with readings of forty degrees—twenty each side of the vertical. The pitch we couldn't measure, but from my porthole I could see the prow of the ship climb repeatedly against the sky, hang there for seconds, then knife down into a volcano of water that rose, curled, and erupted on the foredeck, drowning the winches from view.

Captain Sánchez appeared at dinner and took his place at the head of the main table without a word. He looked grave and liverish, his black eyes swimming in yellow pools veined with red. Until now little about the *Tampico* had seemed Mexican. The regal, ponderously spoken first mate, the Japanese second mate, the austere utilitarianism of the ship's decor—all these had an undefined, international character. But Captain Sánchez was a caricature, a Pancho Villa Mexican right down to his baleen moustache, his hooded eyes, the dissolute mouth, the oily hair, the vanity and dissipation in his swarthy face.

I came down to breakfast a little early the next morning. It had been impossible to sleep. All night the pitch had rammed my head against the cupboard and my feet against the wall, while a corkscrew roll did its best to empty me onto the floor. I could feel nasty stresses and vibrations as the propeller came out of the water, screamed, then bit back into the sea. The dining room looked as though it had been bombed during the night. The tables, bolted to the floor, had stood their ground, but the chairs were swept in a heap on one side of the room. The *Tampico* had a permanent list, driven by the wind on her starboard side.

"A *norte*," the first mate said, showing me how to retrieve a chair, plant myself in it legs apart, and shift against the roll to keep it firm. "A norther. Force Nine now, tomorrow Force Ten.

Maybe Twelve. Enjoy your breakfast. We are all going to be sick!"

The steward announced he couldn't make *huevos rancheros* as he had planned; it was too dangerous to use the galley stove. "Thank God for that!" said Brendan, who took one bite out of a *pan dulce* and bolted. Dominic didn't appear at all. Matthew said his pendulum was reading between sixty-one and sixty-seven degrees; he had fallen out of bed five times. Hail was chattering on the windows, and the sea seemed strangely luminous against a tarnished pewter sky.

I went up to the bridge and instantly gained respect for the truthfulness of the authors I'd read as a boy. The control room had large glass windows on three sides, and from these you could see that the *Tampico* was being tossed about like a lifeboat. The 13,000-ton vessel seemed indeed to have shrunk to lifeboat size, so vast were the ranges of watery alps surrounding her. Where I stood must have been a good forty feet above the waterline, but when the ship slid to the bottom of a trough I could see nothing but piles of water on both sides, swelling above my head. Then one of these mountains would glide beneath the *Tampico* and lift her dizzily up to a summit torn by the gale; and for a long instant she would perch in a nest of spray on the ocean peak. From trough to crest was easily sixty feet.

Captain Sánchez and the second mate were frowning at something. I thought at first it was the row of masts, which waved out of line to one side then the other like leaning fenceposts, as the hull torqued with colossal stresses. But they were watching the deck cargo—the huge steel girder—on the port side. It was mobbed every minute or so by a scrum of water sweeping across the hatches, but in between you could see that it was loose. Several ventilators, upended steel saxophones which stood along the deck, had been flattened like beer cans.

The ship rolled heavily to port, began to climb a swell, and at that moment the steel shifted again, lashing out and wiping ten yards of railing into the sea. There was clearly a risk of losing the girder, and if that happened the *Tampico* would be seriously unbalanced. I remembered stories about shifting cargo; it was usually the beginning of the end.

Captain Sánchez spoke thickly and the second mate went below. Twenty minutes later the first mate and half a dozen seamen were out on deck in oilskins, with rolls of cable and hand winches, and lifelines round their waists. It took them an hour to secure the steel beneath a web of cables—the most heroic manoeuvre I have ever seen. Once, while they were working, the girder scythed across the deck. Most of the men vaulted clear, but one, trapped against a hatch, came within an inch of losing his legs.

At dusk the officers began to celebrate the girder's taming. Captain Sánchez called us over, introduced himself with a funny nod and a limp handshake, and shoved champagne glasses in our hands. It seemed to us that they should have invited the sailors who had done the work, but Mexico, like England, was a hierarchical country (never mind its revolution) and officers didn't socialize with men from below decks. Sometimes the electricians came up to the lounge, but that was as far as it went.

So began the drinking. The storm continued to rise: Force Eleven, Force Twelve, until it peaked at Force Thirteen. (I found out later that Force Thirteen—almost ninety miles per hour—is a hurricane.) The *Tampico*'s roll reached eighty degrees on Matthew's scale and kept that up for twenty-four hours. There was no point in trying to sleep. Even I, the would-be seadog, was feeling seasick now, though I hadn't missed—or lost—a meal. Alcohol, I learned, is a sovereign remedy. I suppose it's because motion sickness is caused by a dispute between your visual horizons and sense of gravity. Drink enough and your internal plumb goes out of whack. End of problem. It was also a good way to stop thinking about being drowned. Or about having offended one's parents, left one's wife. For days I'd stood at the stern, mesmerized by the wake, groggy with diesel fumes, desperately homesick. Hopelessly so, for there was really nothing to go back to. Home for the last few months had been a rented cellar in Cambridge, damp and dark, with a musty single bed where the nurse and I wrestled with the cold. I missed her; I missed watching Monty Python on her friends' TV. I missed the Mitre, our local pub, the pie and chips and four pints of beer that were my usual dinner. I even missed the building job I'd taken to pay for this meagre independence. An image of a life I might have led sprang on me sometimes when my guard was down: a stolid brick house with a fence and flowerbed, a Ph.D on the wall, a wife, children. Wasn't that what you were supposed to be when you grew up? At such moments I longed for the massive engine to throw a rod, hole a piston, knock out a bearing, so the *Tampico* would have to turn and limp back to the nearest European port. But the engine kept to its harsh rhythm; the ship kept ploughing her furrow across the world.

The Mexicans were generous with their duty-free supplies. With no expense and no hindrance I drank like a drain. We all did (except Matthew), but God, how *I* drank. Each morning, when the alcohol turned sour in your stomach, there were a few bleak hours, but the answer of course was to start drinking again at lunch and press on undaunted through the day, through the storm of hangover to the port of euphoria, and on to the eye of the hurricane where one passed out in bliss. We knocked back tequila. First the salt to make you thirsty, next the rancid shot of distilled maguey juice, then the lime to take the taste away. We chased it with beer—Dos Equis, which came in brown bottles from Cervecería Moctezuma (note the spelling). This, we agreed, was Project Moctezuma.

I was usually the last of the *ingleses* to reach oblivion. In the small hours, somebody would drag me out of the dining room, and I would wake up later on a bench beneath steel stairs, the engines booming in my head, my eyes blasted by a neon tube in a wire cage. I'd crawl to my cabin on all fours, at the lowest point, the moment when you feel you haven't a friend in the world—least of all yourself. One morning, after such a night, I looked in the mirror and saw I was losing my hair.

During the days of storm and uproar, the ship had been hove to, pointed into the weather with the screw turning just enough to keep her under control. At least I assume she was—all the officers seemed to be drinking all the time, and when I asked who was running the ship they laughed and said, "Captain Radar," pointing up to the dish or perhaps to God.

When the storm at last died down a certain amount of decorum returned. Ice fell from masts and booms, a gentle rain washed the salt from our windows, and the roll settled to a trifling twenty degrees, then fifteen. We flung open doors and portholes. Dr. Johnson's jail became an open prison with the prospect of early release. I had been cooped up for so long that I got sore muscles just walking up and down the deck. Seagulls appeared, and Captain Sánchez shot at them from the roof of the bridge with a large revolver. I didn't see him hit one. We passed one of the Bahamas, lying on the horizon like a whale. The water became smooth and glaucous, reflecting a metallic sheen from the sky, which wore a thin veil of high, torn cloud. You could feel the foul weather lurking somewhere, hoping to make a comeback as a tropical storm. The ocean looked as oily and deceptive as a diplomat.

"Tomorrow is the *santo* of Captain Sánchez!" The first mate had a conspiratorial tone. I understood his words but I didn't know what they meant. Some sort of embarrassing Catholic ritual involving a plaster saint?

"*Santo*?"

"It is like his birthday. But it is the day of his saint. The day of the saint for whom he is named. We are going to honour him with a celebration."

"What saint would that be?" I asked. "We heretics don't...."

"San Hilario!" The second mate raised a sparse Oriental eyebrow, as if I'd never heard of Christmas Day.

"So!" said Brendan in a stage whisper. "Captain Hilary Sánchez! If I had a handle like that I'd keep quiet about it."

"Hilarious," said Dominic, the Etonian, icily.

On January 13th—St. Hilary's day—we did not see the captain. At dinner time the officers were sitting round the table as usual, talking quietly. There didn't seem to be any religious preparations. Perhaps the captain's *santo* had been some kind of joke.

The steward was back on form. He had swept up the broken crockery and scraped the mess from the galley floor, and tonight had made *guajolote en mole*, turkey in a sauce of chiles, almonds, sesame seeds, and unsweetened chocolate. My three fellows prodded their black platefuls suspiciously and made scatalogical remarks. I told them this was an Aztec delicacy, rather like curry. From it rose a rich fragrance, a strange harmony of spices mingled with boiled bird and the chalky smell of fresh tortillas. With the calm weather their appetites had returned and they were soon won over.

At about nine o'clock, Captain Sánchez came out of his cabin and took his place, rather late. A plate of *mole* quickly disappeared, as if devoured by his moustache. The steward brought us all dessert—individual crème caramels, known in Mexico as *flan*. Suddenly the first mate clapped his hands and yelled, "Champagne for Don Hilario!" And the captain, guessing from this version of his name what was afoot, could hardly contain his glee.

After every round of champagne, each officer made a speech. The second mate punctilious, very Japanese; the engineer shy, grave, and tongue-tied. The first mate was the star, a master of the Latin style of oratory. So lofty was his language that many of the words lay beyond my ken, but he spoke so slowly and expressively that I could get the drift. He humbly begged the *Tampico*'s esteemed captain to accept this imperfect little *homenaje*, this homage, from his subordinates. Words could not express the loyalty and gratitude that thrived in the heart of every man aboard. He knew that the English guests—he gave a gracious bow in our direction and motioned for the steward to fill our glasses—though incapable of expressing themselves adequately in the Spanish idiom, shared his sentiments, and indeed had insisted that he convey them on this special, fortunate day.

And so it went on. Not merely one speech from each officer, but as many rounds of speeches as there were bottles of champagne: Don Hilario, the great navigator, deliverer from many a storm such as the one we had just witnessed! Don Hilario, specially favoured and protected by the wise and miraculous St. Hilary! Don Hilario, the model family man, a father figure to all aboard! Don Hilario, the finest captain in the service of the merchant marine of Mexico!

With each encomium all charged their glasses, raised them, and shouted in one voice, "*¡Viva el capitán!*" The cry would waken the captain, who had become prone to narcolepsy. He would nod, as if to acknowledge his admirers' shrewd judgement of character, and grin fatly round the table with enormous satisfaction.

At length, like a king dismissing sycophantic courtiers, Captain Sánchez whispered something in the steward's ear and wobbled into his cabin. I thought that was the last we'd see of him. But he came back out with a cardboard box under one arm and a film projector in his hand. The steward made us all get up, pushed the chairs in a semicircle, and unfurled a screen on the wall. Sánchez, puffing and sighing with concentration, managed to thread a reel and switch on. He said something about wanting to repay his gallant crew for their kindness and loyalty by entertaining them with these moments that he himself "had captured at many of the world's great cities and most famous touristic destinations."

The films were exactly as we feared: Captain Sánchez with his family—a defeated-looking woman in a fur coat, a porcine son of about fourteen in a grey flannel suit, and a vain little nine-year-old girl dressed like a doll in floral prints and lace and gypsy earrings. There they were on the Champs-Elysées, on top of the Eiffel Tower, before the Colosseum, beside the Copenhagen mermaid, at the Leaning Tower of Pisa. It was dismal eight-millimetre stuff, black and white, grainy, covered in motes and scratches, with unintended *contre-jour* and the Sánchez family abruptly walking up walls and on their heads. The lounge was thrown open to the lower ranks for the show. The men had come in obsequiously, perching on every tabletop and squatting on the floor. After three or four reels they began to drift away with mumbles of *muchas gracias.*

Undaunted, Don Hilario fished yet another reel from the cardboard box. He said nothing at all. We were slow to notice that something was different. In our drunkenness we were like a drowsy congregation who miss an *outré* remark in the midst of a boring sermon. I remember thinking that the movie stars had changed. I didn't know Sánchez had an elder daughter. But hang on, that's not the captain, and what are they doing taking off their clothes? And that isn't the Leaning Tower of Pisa. An erect penis had appeared. It bobbed in close-up, menacingly, like a truncheon in your face. It seemed about to speak. It was suddenly eclipsed by a gibbous breast with a nipple the size of a fried egg.

These movies were probably only a few years old, bought in Denmark or Holland, yet they had the flickering, archival quality of early films. They were silent, but you could almost hear panting and gasps. The lighting was bluish and dim, but the illumination would rise without warning, casting a remorseless glare on stained wallpaper, sagging grey underwear, and the wrinkled soles of dirty feet. They were little better, technically, than the captain's holiday reels; you felt you were watching something filmed through a keyhole by police. They were *echt* blue films.

The show was a wild success. The captain won back his audience and doubled it. The lounge filled with tobacco smoke and human heat. Cases of "Project Moctezuma" were consumed. We laughed until the chocolate turkey, as Brendan dubbed it, threatened to take flight, though some of the crew took the show more seriously, hushing at moments of orgasm as if to catch the silent grunts and moans. Others whistled and called out instant reviews. *¡Qué bonita!* to a blonde twice my age. *¡Qué huevos!* (What balls!) at a frantic little man in bed with twins.

The show ended when Captain Sánchez, unable to endure any more celebration of his *santo*—let alone thread another reel—crawled off to his cabin on all fours.

Next morning. The early sun, reflected through my porthole by the glass of a boom operator's cab, splashed a pink rose of light on the cabin wall. The rose moved up and down with the gentle heave of the ship. I lay in my bunk, wondering how I'd feel if I stood up. When the rose turned orange and started groping across the floor I dressed and went outside for air. Sailors were already out, scraping the decks and painting them brown. An arc welder flashed like a variable star at the scene of the girder's revolt. I went forward and leant over the bow, inhaling the oyster smell of the Gulf Stream. For the first time the sea seemed warm, light, tropical. Flying fish, chased by dolphins, shot from the *Tampico*'s wash.

Tension lingered in the atmosphere. The veil of cloud was still with us, far above, and it stayed all day, leaching colour from the seascape. At dusk the ceiling thickened and descended until it hung no more than a hundred feet above the water. Both sea and sky were perfectly still, perfectly flat. As darkness fell, a glow surrounded the ship and stretched behind her like a monarch's train. The glow came from the water, from phosphorescence blooming in our wake and at the bow, in any disturbance of the glossy sea. Matthew, who knew everything, said it was caused by millions of tiny creatures. I went to the head (which used seawater), shut the door, switched off the electricity, and flushed. The bowl filled with a torrent of ghostly light.

For the next two days we sailed the smooth waters of the Gulf under a fierce sun and pure blue sky. We could smell Mexico long before we saw it. A moist offshore breeze carried the spoor of a hot and ancient land: blossoms, skunky vegetation, woodsmoke, a faint tang of swamps or shit. Gulls invaded the bridge, and insects danced in the navigation lights. Sixteen days after leaving the Old World we sighted the New.

In mid-afternoon the *Tampico* steamed into Veracruz—place of the True Cross—where Cortés had landed in 1519. Here he and his men had been watched by spies, studied by envoys, and drawn by artists sent down to the coast from Mexico City by a panicky Moctezuma. Only a squadron of *zopilotes* came to watch us—black turkey vultures with bald, saurian heads and cynical eyes. They circled until we slowed enough for an easy landing on the rail. Then they alighted and sat like dissolute priests at a cockfight, jostling for a view. When the cooks finished tossing out the day's offal from the galley the *zopilotes* dropped to the deck, wings arched, and picked the place clean in minutes.

After his *santo*, the captain had reverted to his Ahab role for the rest of the voyage. But he came out to greet the customs and immigration officers with a case of schnapps. He saw to it that our passports were stamped with no fuss and handed them back to us himself.

"I say goodbye from my ship and welcome to my country!" Captain Sánchez said with a cheerful handshake. Then a frown crossed his face.

"You are *jóvenes muy correctos*. . . ." He searched for the right words in English. "Young men berry berry well-behave. I hope you forgive our little fiestas here. At head office they not understand the life. . . . The life of the sea!"

He gave each of us a sudden embrace and waved us down the gangplank.

"Have a good time in *México!*" he roared.

Though I didn't know it then, England would never again be my home.

TWO

Condor

From Mexico I went to Canada, to the University of Calgary, where I did graduate work with the vague idea of getting a doctorate. I dropped out after a year or two, having learned I was temperamentally unsuited for the academic life. But I stayed on there, working as a truck driver, progressing from small vans to a forty-ton Kenworth with eighteen wheels. I would save up money and travel on the proceeds. My first big trip was overland from Canada to Peru. It began in an old Austin I bought for $75, which got me as far as Costa Rica. From there I took a bus to Panama, and a short flight to Medellín, Colombia, already a dangerous town but nothing like it is now. I hitchhiked most of the way through the former Inca Empire, down the spine of the Ecuadorean and Peruvian Andes, along the desert coast. From northern Chile I turned up into the mountains, through La Paz, Bolivia, back into Peru, along the shore of Lake Titicaca, and over the continental divide to the goal of my pilgrimage: Cusco, the ancient Inca capital.

In the same school library that had supplied me with nautical tales there had been a Victorian boys' novel called *Manco, The Peruvian Chief*, written by W.H.G. Kingston, a prolific author who lived in Peru during the 1860s. It was this book, not the sea stories, that would shape my life. Set during the great rebellion of 1780, when Tupa Amaru II, a direct descendant of the last Inca king, came close to restoring Indian rule in the Andes, *Manco* evoked a "lost" civilization and the plight of its heirs. The story appealed to me all the more because I'd been taught nothing about South America at school. It was my own discovery. When I reached Peru—more than a century after Kingston—I found that the essentials of the place he had described were little changed. Modern Peru is still a divided land in which the descendants of conquered and conqueror endlessly refight the Spanish conquest.

For the rest of my twenties I drove trucks, tried farming (a failure), travelled without notes—easygoing years of wanderlust and casual experiment when one felt indestructible and time seemed as ample as the world. Soon after turning thirty, I was knocked flat on my back by a bad case of hepatitis in Peru. It was my third or fourth trip there—I forget which—and it felt as if it might be my last. When I got home I was too weak for physical work; the slow convalescence gave me time to think about alternatives, and about my life. The old desire to write returned, and I decided to try a travel book. *Cut Stones and Crossroads: A Journey in Peru* was published three years later.

Like many a new author, I thought publication would bring instant wealth. But though the book was well received on both sides of the Atlantic, the royalties couldn't keep me very long. I began writing for radio and magazines while working on a second book. "Condor", which was broadcast on CBC Radio, is a modern echo of the conflict that began when Pizarro seized Atawallpa in 1532. Sometimes bloody, sometimes an uneasy stalemate, Peru's five-hundred-year war is most of all a cultural war.

I SUPPOSE EVERYONE gets the bullfight he deserves. My first was in Mexico City. I had gone hoping for a spectacle like the one in D.H. Lawrence's *Plumed Serpent.* A spoilsport by nature, I wasn't wearing a straw hat for fellow spectators to seize; nor did I have a bald spot to tempt a well-aimed orange. Mexicans sat on either side of me, fidgeting with excitement and trying to drink red wine from a *bota.* They offered me some. It dripped from our chins like the blood that appeared at the bull's mouth after the picadors had done their work.

The climax was a disgrace. Stab, stab, stab went the matador's sword, but he failed to find the yielding spot between the vertebrae. There was no sudden convulsion; no satisfying ejaculation of blood. An attendant walked into the arena, pulled out a revolver, and shot the bull through the head.

I swore I would never go again. But years later, in a village near the peak of Ausangate in the Andes of Peru, I saw a very different bullfight: a fight between a bull and a bird.

It's about nine o'clock in the morning when I reach Wayramarka—a huddle of stone walls and adobe houses at 14,000 feet—after walking uphill for three hours from the nearest road. The sun still lies behind the summit of Ausangate; grey light pours over the treeless landscape from a hole in the sky. There is no wind—a blessing—and the village feels hemmed in by the mountain's shadow, by cliffs like coalfaces, by a glacier like a flock of dirty sheep.

High above, perhaps half-way to the peak, a condor sails without a flap, its wing-feathers and Elizabethan ruff flashing white as it turns. In Inca times a condor was believed to carry the sun across the sky each day, just as a puma made the return journey through the underworld at night. And for the royal Incas, who claimed descent from the sun, the condor was a family totem. It did not trouble them that the bird is in fact a vulture; they revered it as the greatest creature of the upper world.

The streets of Wayramarka are already filling with the Bruegelish filth and clutter of an Andean fiesta. The smell of dung, human and animal, is waking from the frost. Women in black skirts, red shawls, and lampshade hats trot along barefoot, hunched beneath sacks of boiled potatoes and roast guinea-pigs. Men in brown ponchos and scarecrow fedoras are pissing drunkenly against a wall. A wave of a bottle, a red face, and a mischievous, unfocused gaze: "*Gringu!* Where do you come from? What brings you here?"

The wind blows down from the slopes below the glacier, rippling the llama pastures, raising dust in the village, rustling the roofs—untidy scalps of grass held down by hairnets weighted with stones. It brings drifts of different melodies: a chaotic brass band weaving in and out of key; a flute solo; gusts of panpipe music accompanied by the cardiac beat of a large drum. I come to a corral at the end of a street where men are blowing cornets made of cowhorns nested in one another like paper cups. Women are beating tambourines and shrilling, in the Inca language, a thin piercing song:

Turu turullay, turu,
Tayta Apu chaskikusunki....

(Oh bull, my little bull,
May the Mountain Lord receive you....)

In a corner stands the bull, a black beast with lyre horns, tied to a boulder by a rawhide lasso. It has ropes around its midriff, as if for a small saddle. An orange trickle falls from its tasselled penis and steams on the frozen earth. The women stop their song and call out, thinking I won't understand. "Pooh! Shitarse bull, what are you frightened of? Maybe this gringo is after your balls."

I ask what the girths are for.

"*Kunturpaq!*" the women shriek, surprised: "For the condor!"

There's nothing for it but to have a drink in the nearest bar—a shop stocked with rusty sardine tins, soda pop, and a forty-five-gallon drum of cane alcohol *licor*. The shopkeeper bends to the tap at the bottom of the drum and fills a shot glass, which I chase with Coca-Cola. He is an elderly mestizo and his name is Don Ramón. His face resembles a frostbitten potato, and on it he wears a grizzled stubble to advertise his Spanish genes. (Indians have scanty beards, and what they have they pluck.) No, señor, he is not a fleabitten *indio*. And he doesn't approve of these *indio* bullfights, which the government outlawed years ago, even though, he has to admit, they are good for business. "These Indians don't even speak Castilian," he adds in a low voice. "*¡No saben castellano, carajo! Son gente inculta, salvajes, ignorantes.*" Then he looks at me with accusation in his small, quick eyes: "Why do you gringos come here? This is not Peru. If you want to see a real bullfight, go to Lima, señor. Why, in Lima they bring the matadors and even the bulls themselves from Spain!"

"Where is this bull from?"

"From up there." He lifts his chin towards the mountain. "From the high pastures near the snow line—it is always that way. These people have many superstitions, they believe that a *sallqa turu*, a wild bull, comes out of the mountain itself, from the icy lake below the glacier. Pah!" While he talks he bustles in the shop, arranging tins, counting change, squinting at the girlie calendar on the wall, dabbing at the counter with a filthy rag, as if to emphasize by these actions his membership in Western civilization. But his poncho is as ragged as any worn by the poorest Indians and his patched trousers stink. I think: He looks like a mummy—the sort found in desert graves: brown shrunken cadavers, worm-eaten around the eyes, which nevertheless seem to require only a little water to return to life.

I buy a second drink. The *licor* flames in my stomach and spreads down my legs, where it meets the warmth of the sun now climbing from behind the glacier and casting an orange bloom on the mud floor. The brass band comes down the street: men wearing balaclavas and bright woollen pixie hats with earflaps—both together—blowing into battered instruments, their cheeks puffed and veined like bladders.

I walk outside and understand instantly why the Incas worshipped the sun. Its rays are strong now, but every shadow is a frozen outpost of the night. The band turns the corner and quickly dies. At these altitudes sound carries clearly in a line of sight, but is lost behind an obstacle. Then the breathy tooting of panpipes reasserts itself and draws me to the village plaza. The square has been prepared for the bullfight, its perimeter tiered with planks and adobe bricks. The benches are already filled, mainly by women sitting regally on their layers of homespun skirts; latecomers are perching on walls, rooftops, even on the flimsy barrier of wood and corrugated iron that forms the ring itself.

Inside the ring a dozen pipers are rotating slowly in a circle. Their pipes, like miniature organs, range from a few inches in length to three or four feet; two men beat drums as large as themselves. The music is hoarse and vigorous, a tautly orchestrated rasping and hooting that seems to originate deep within the Indians' barrel chests and reverberate from the ice and rock and crystalline air pressing down upon the tiny settlement.

Two men dressed in brown vicuña ponchos with rainbow stripes call to me, patting a space of bench beside them. "*Gringu*," they shout. "Come and sit. Come and drink." The short chubby one introduces himself as Don Felipe Maywa. The other has a broad bony face with a natural grin and a cheek bulging with a wad of coca leaves. His name is Wilfredo Qoriwaman. They wave a bottle of *licor* invitingly. It would be bad form to refuse. Among the Incas, ceremonial drinking of corn beer was a solemn act; and their descendants have added cane spirit to the ritual. In an account of the Spanish conquest written by a nephew of the Inca emperor, the Spaniards' refusal to drink with Atawallpa at their first meeting (because they suspected poison) was taken as an unpardonable insult. In return, Atawallpa threw down the Bible offered him. So began the mutual rejection of Europe and Peru.

The panpipers file out of the ring to make way for yet another band: three violins and a harp carried aloft on the harpist's shoulder. Men in feathered cloaks and bird masks follow. Among them is a live condor, held by the outstretched wings. The bird must be twelve feet in span, with a deep chest and powerful neck, its white ruff puffed in anger. It glares at its captors with vigilant reptilian eyes, and shakes a crimson wattle. After a while the condor seems resigned to being frogmarched around the arena, its talons clenched and trailing like the feet of a dead crow. I wonder if it is wounded or in shock. Then someone pours a shot of *licor* down its beak, and I realize it is merely as drunk as everybody else.

Maywa and Qoriwaman tell me how such birds are caught. Sometimes a man will wait for hours, even days, beneath a cowhide spread over a crevice in the rocks. When a condor lands he grabs it by the feet, counting on the hide to protect him from the beak until the bird is subdued. A safer method is to throw an animal carcass down in a hollow and wait on horseback some way off. When several condors have gathered and begun to dispute their find, the horsemen, if quick enough, can rush in with a net. They explain all this with much flapping of ponchos, stirring the smokiness of their windowless houses into the atmosphere of *licor* and dust rising from the dancing men and bird.

I remember an essay by the anthropologist Clifford Geertz. He analysed Balinese cockfighting as what he called "deep play", a performance full of symbolic statements about the things most admired, and most feared, by that society: "As much of America surfaces in a ball park... or around a poker table," Geertz said, "much of Bali surfaces in a cock ring. For it is only apparently cocks that are fighting there. Actually, it is men."

Bullfighting may go back to the fertility rites of the Minoans. On murals at Knossos in Crete, bare-breasted young women seize bulls by the horns and vault gracefully over their backs. At Neolithic sites in Anatolia, you can see much earlier shrines decorated with rows of modelled horns and women's breasts. When Christianity triumphed over the old gods of Europe, these cults were transformed into the familiar Iberian sport. Woman lost her part in the ritual; the acrobatics of the Bronze Age became a loaded fight to the death between matador and bull—a contest of machismo and a symbolic slaying of the pagan world. It isn't difficult to see the strutting, preening bullfighters in the same light in which Geertz saw the fighting cocks of Bali: "Self-operating penises, ambulant genitals with a life of their own."

The matador, gaudy and tumescent, achieves fatal rape of the horned one. Pan, the old god of the wilds, is dispatched in a shudder and a spurt of blood. It is essentially a snuff film.

The bull trots into the ring to a great cheer from the crowd. I see that Don Ramón and other mestizos have taken prominent seats. The shopkeeper is waving his fedora in one hand and a bottle in the other. He has forgotten that he doesn't approve. Three men jump down and begin to shake their ponchos at the bull. After a few circuits of the ring, the animal understands it is trapped, and turns on its pursuers. One man throws his poncho over the bull's face, trips, and falls down. Shouts of "*¡Carajo! Drunkard!*" Things are too easy for the bull, for the crowd's sense of fair play. The spectators light firecrackers and throw them into the ring. The bull, now assailed by half a dozen fighters, runs wildly from side to side, tossing its head. It clips one man in the ribs and knocks him spinning against the barrier. Blood runs down the corrugated iron and onto the dirt.

Don Felipe hands me the bottle. "Good!" he says. It looks to him like a good "blood fiesta". "Last year," he explains, "five men were hurt and the crops were full." For the Indians, human—not merely bovine—blood must be spilled. It is man's payment to the earth and mountain gods for the life made possible by the mystery of fertility.

After first blood, a horseman lassoes the bull. The violins and harp emerge from a side street. The dancers with the condor return. They have adorned the bird's wings with coloured ribbons; now they tie its feet to the bull's girth. Bird and bull are released. They stand for a second, gazing at the crowd. Then the condor smells blood and strains to jump down. A firecracker lands under the bull, making it buck and kick its hind legs in the air. The condor grimly keeps its balance, like an elderly but determined tourist on a camel; then, seeming to realize what is needed, begins beating the bull's flanks with powerful wings. This only increases the bucking, but the condor proves to be an agile cowboy. Three more men jump into the ring; a homemade rocket whizzes over the bird and explodes against the barrier. The condor, thoroughly alarmed, takes a bite out of the bull's ear; the bull charges the men and knocks one down. The man limps away. The condor begins to peck at the bull's neck, striking and tugging with a beak designed for ripping leathery carcasses. Soon rivulets of blood are running down the bull's dewlap and darkening the dust like blots of ink. The mestizos are ecstatic. "*¡Mira como pica!*" they shout. "Look how he pecks!" For them the condor is merely a substitute for the mounted picadors of Spain. For the Indians, the condor's role is more subtle.

The Andean universe, both ancient and modern, is structured by a system of complementary opposites rather like the Chinese yin and yang. The two halves are called "upper" and "lower", though they may or may not have anything to do with actual height. Sun, day, man, birds, fire, and mountains belong to the upper half; moon, night, woman, wild beasts, water, lowlands, and sea belong to the lower. Wild bulls, "born" from the mountain tarns, are identified in myth with older denizens of the lower world, especially the puma; they are often given feline names. Certain unifying principles transcend the upper and lower divide. One of these is the "bird-feline", a mythological beast that first appears in Peruvian art more than three thousand years ago. The condor and bull are, among other things, this composite creature, formed from both halves of the world and called into being as an agent of the Andean gods.

The rampage of the winged, four-footed beast continues until another man is badly hurt. The bull's horn tears open his thigh, and the condor manages to seize a forearm raised in defence. Bleeding from both wounds, the amateur toreador, fortunately well anaesthetized with coca and *licor*, is carried away by his friends. A languid calm falls on the arena. The sun, so weak when low, now blazes at the zenith, draining the colour from spectators' clothes, drying the blood on the earth. The offerings, it seems, have been accepted.

Two men approach the panting animals warily. They untie the condor, give it a long draught of beer, lift it to their shoulders, and bear it away like a drunken king. The violins play a slow *kacharpari* of farewell. Indians begin to leave their seats and follow the procession. The condor, drunk, tired, bruised perhaps, but above all honoured, will now be carried up the mountain to the place where it was caught.

The fate of the bull is less glorious. The bull is always the loser. The sublime totality of the bird-feline dissolves at the end of the fight. The upper world emerges victorious, as it should. The bull is led to slaughter.

But that is not all.

When the Spaniards came to Peru they soon recognized the power of the condor as a symbol of the sun and Inca kings. To desecrate the bird they would string one up from a gallows by its feet and race by on horseback, pummelling it to death with mailed fists.

The condor bullfight is the Andean world's revenge. As in the Balinese cockfight, it is really men who are engaged: Incas against the invading race. In death and defeat the bull returns to being the familiar symbol of Spain and the Hispanic Peruvians who dominate the Andes from their city of Lima on the coast. The condor's victory is a victory over history, a reversal of the conquest, a symbolic righting of the world.

Felipe Maywa rises unsteadily to join the condor's entourage. "Come," he says. "Come along and celebrate." He offers a swig from his bottle, and as I drink he lifts his chin to point towards the bird.

"Sometimes," he says, "we see condors from earlier years—still flying the ribbons from their wings."

THREE

The Lamanai Enigma

Not long after *Cut Stones and Crossroads* came out, I moved from Alberta, where I'd had a tiny wooden house with a view of the Rockies (if you climbed on the roof), to Toronto.

By February 1985 I was near the end of my second book, *On Fiji Islands*, inhabiting a tropical inner landscape painfully at odds with my new surroundings. I hadn't taken well to Toronto's six-month purgatory of grey, damp, grimy cold. Housing was tight, and in haste I'd rented a flat on the twenty-fifth floor of a tower block overlooking two freeways. Trucks vibrated my middle ear all night; police sirens invaded my dreams; all the windows faced north. The sun hadn't looked in since September. Wind was another matter—at this height it came in with the slightest encouragement. If you opened any window a crack, even in mild weather, the wind hissed and wailed like heretics burning at the stake. And every evening, at exactly five, a reek of fried onions filled the whole building.

I was having trouble with the last chapter. I hadn't slept soundly for weeks. I was almost out of my mind. A doctor gave me some pills which only made things worse (they have since been banned for causing psychotic reactions).

Then the phone rang, and it was the geographical magazine *Equinox* offering me a trip to Belize, formerly British Honduras. Belize wasn't a favourite place of mine. On my only visit there—during my long trip south in the old Austin—I'd been skilfully robbed within minutes of reaching the capital. Whenever I heard the word Belize, I thought of Sergeant Bliss.

"Write your story down there, maan," Sergeant Bliss had said to me that night in Belize City. He was a very large Creole policeman and his forefinger was thumping a sheet of paper, like a labrador's tail on the floor. But he did not look friendly.

"Begin at de beginning: *At approximately 7:30 p.m. on the evening of May sixth, 1970, I was dining at Mom's Triangle Bar when I observed....*" It was a strenuous imitation of a London copper.

"What's the point of this?" I said. "My car's just been broken into. Minutes ago. I've been robbed. And I'd be very grateful if you'd do something about it." I'd driven across the United States and Mexico with no more trouble than a couple of flat tyres. I wanted to carry on through the rest of Central America, park the car, and fly to Colombia. Now all my travellers' cheques were gone.

I went through the story again, loudly this time—for the benefit of any superiors who might be lurking in a back office. In those days Belize was still British. *I* was still British. If I could get past this local sergeant to a British officer something would be done.

An American had warned me about Belize: *Watch your stuff—they're good down there.* He'd had a pistol stolen from beneath his pillow while he slept on it. That was impressive; I was on my guard. The Austin's boot, reinforced with a steel hasp and an expensive padlock, had seemed the safest place to leave my gear while I ate. Even so, I stepped outside the restaurant every few minutes to check. But between these patrols someone had expertly picked the lock, grabbed my bag, and run off up the street. I followed a trail of my belongings in the gutter, with the rifled backpack at the end. Luckily it was money they were after—I found my passport in a puddle with my underwear.

When I caught sight of the Central Police Station, a prim clapboard building on stilts, my spirits rose. It had the familiar blue lantern over the door and some bobbies' bikes leaning against a picket fence. A few words with a chap in a crisp tropical uniform and all would be well.

The first I saw of Sergeant Bliss were his feet, on the desk. He got up laboriously, filling the room, an enormous genie with bloodshot eyes. Bibs of sweat stained his chest and underarms. His breath was a blast of rum.

"Yes?"

"My car has been broken into on the street."

I gave the details. When I'd finished he said nothing at all.

"Aren't you going to do anything about it?"

He sighed and walked slowly to a filing cabinet, returning with the sheet of paper.

"Write your story down there, maan."

"There must be people on the street at this moment who saw it happen. Eyewitnesses. Aren't you going to investigate?"

"We'll investigate it in de mawning, maan."

"I'd like to speak to the British officer in charge."

Sergeant Bliss sighed again, walked slowly to the filing cabinet, and came back triumphantly with another sheet of paper.

"You can write him a letter, maan."

Equinox's offer—to cover a dig by the Royal Ontario Museum at an ancient Maya city "in the jungle"—would have been more enticing if the jungle hadn't been in Belize. But I needed the work. Most of all I needed a change.

BELIZE STILL HAS one of those romantic airports where, instead of being excreted through an aluminium catheter, you walk off the plane down a ladder and across acres of blistering tarmac. You feel the sun, smell the air (a hot bath of jet fuel and swamp gas), you have a sense of arrival. Alan Carruthers—a photographer—and I were struggling with a surfeit of duty-free hand luggage bought in Miami when we'd changed planes. We'd been told not to arrive in the jungle empty-handed. Alan had wanted to add a ghetto-blaster minutes before takeoff, but I'd persuaded him that a dozen wine bottles, several quarts of scotch, and a thousand cigarettes were probably enough.

We felt, and looked, like pale larvae accidentally exposed to the sun. Everyone else in the terminal building was black or tan, in beach shirts and sandals; I still had a goosedown jacket over my arm. A sign reminded "entertainers and boxers" that they needed an exit paper, another advertised the attractions of "local dinning [*sic*] and hanging out." A map revealed our destination: Lamanai, also called Indian Church, on the New River lagoon thirty or forty miles to the northwest. Around us bubbled a gumbo of Caribbean English.

Customs officer to Alan: "How many bottles, maan?"

Wright to customs officer: "We're with the Royal Ontario Museum."

Baggage handler to me: "Give I ten dollahs."

Customs officer: "Too *moch*, maan. Far too moch!"

Baggage handler: "You no give I ten dollahs 'cos you tink I a niggah!"

Customs officer: "I mean the bottles, maan. You got too moch."

Then the officer spied Alan's equipment. Two metal cases, two canvas kit bags, a tripod and reflector inside plastic tubes the size of large-calibre bazookas.

"We'll have to take a look at all that. You better come into the office and make a list."

"I've got one ready," said Alan, waving a typed sheet. The officer looked disappointed.

"That's no good. You got to use the proper forms."

It seemed the right time to drop a name.

"Will this take long?" I asked. "Charles Usher's supposed to be meeting us here."

"Charlie? You know Charlie?" I explained that Charlie was flying us into the bush. "Why didn't you say so, maan? No problem. Away you go." The customs officer was all smiles. Belize is small enough that everybody knows a somebody. Charlie was the prime minister's nephew.

He appeared on cue.

"Heel Bunk?" he said, and I had to think for a second. Of course, Hill Bank, the airstrip near the ruins.

There was just room for the equipment, the booze, and us in Charlie's tiny plane. Twenty minutes later we thumped down on the gravel at Hill Bank, which was merely one end of a logging trail that ran from the New River Lagoon through uninhabited forest to a place called Gallon Jug. It seemed deserted, half a dozen clapboard bunkhouses in a clearing overlooking a lake. Herons and snail kites were gliding above the shallows. The jungle smelled like an armpit. In the nearest patch of weeds was an old traction engine with a termite nest in the boiler. Beyond it a *zopilote* buzzard watched us hopefully from a dead tree. We were in the middle of nowhere, and it had taken only ten hours to get here from Toronto.

A dark-haired, well-tanned white man appeared over the crest of the bank and introduced himself in a Quebec accent. He was

Claude Bélanger, assistant to David Pendergast, the dig director. "You look like ghosts," he said, and led us down to a carious jetty whose remaining timbers jumped beneath our feet like xylophone keys. We got into the museum's speedboat for the final leg to the ruins. Claude gunned the big outboard, throwing us back in the seats. Warm spray and tiny insects splattered on my teeth, and I felt as if the last six months of northern cold and grime were a long paralysis from which I had just been released.

The lagoon is a dilation of the New River, a blue sausage on the map, about a mile wide and twelve miles long, before the river contracts again and winds like an intestine through the swamps below Orange Walk and Corozal to the Caribbean. On the far shore, pools of flooded vegetation steamed in the evening sunlight. "Crocodiles," said Claude gaily, adding that Lamanai, the Maya name of the ruined city, meant either "submerged crocodile" or "drowned insect."

We had sped north for about fifteen minutes when Claude pointed at a range of heavily forested hills stretching for about two miles along the western shore. "Lamanai," he said, a hint of awe in his voice. These hills—I noticed now their regular silhouettes—were overgrown buildings.

Travelling in a place where the past outshines the present is always a humbling and philosophical experience. Belizeans are perversely fond of pointing out that the tallest building in the country is still the great pyramid at Xunantunich (shoe-nun-two-*nitch*), which overlooks the Guatemalan border like a craggy watchtower. At more than 130 feet, it is rivalled only by a 112-foot pyramid at Lamanai. Similarly, the Belizean population was far greater when these cities thrived in the first millennium than it is today—perhaps five or ten times the present number of 150,000.

Alan opened one of his metal boxes and—*welcome to Belize*—the telephoto lens he wanted had disappeared. So had a good flash unit and one or two other expensive pieces of glass. Where could it have happened? At Miami? Between plane and customs at Belize? Alan was a big man, made even bigger by his green fishing vest crammed with film and filters. His red hair and untidy beard promised a stormy nature, but he kept his cool. "I've never worried before and never lost a thing. I must have been overdue for this." He didn't mention it again.

Lamanai camp resembled a genteel hunting lodge: trim thatched huts in the round-cornered Maya style among clumps of hibiscus and flamboyant, all shaded by imposing trees. A grassy slope met the water in a fringe of reeds. The archaeologists had used rubble from the dig to build a long jetty, and at the end of this stood a boathouse thatched with palm leaves like an Acapulco beer stall. David Pendergast was standing there to meet the boat. Belize had toasted him the colour of a potsherd since I'd last seen him in Toronto. With thick hair, albeit greying, he seemed much younger than his fifty years, his youthful mien enhanced by a punky shirt with the sleeves cut off at the shoulders.

It was already getting dark under the trees; the sun had fallen behind the ruins but scrawny palmettos and dyewoods on the far shore still burned with its last rays. Small frogs mewed like kittens in the reeds, and again the breeze carried that skunky whiff of the forest. A distant generator began to throb; lights came on in the huts. It was time for dinner and a bottle or two of Belikin, Belize's only beer, whose label features the main pyramid at Altun Ha, a Maya ruin dug and consolidated by Pendergast in the 1960s.

Pendergast runs a tight ship: meals are served at six, noon, and six, *sharp*. In the larger hut that doubles as kitchen and dining room, the table was spread with meat loaf, steaming potatoes, and a fresh tomato salad—handiwork of the chief cook, Doña Lupa. The meal was followed by cookies and tea, and it would have been hard to imagine oneself in the heart of Belize were it not for the tarantula discovered in the teapot. "That's all right," Pendergast said. "They don't drink much."

David Pendergast is a natural talker, intoxicated by words, endlessly informative on anything from archaeology to cookery, opera to children's books. A magnetic field of smile lines circles his eyes, and his gaze explores a middle distance filled with anecdotes and ideas. This was not an after-dinner conversation but a performance; he spoke as if rehearsed, in grammatically faultless paragraphs, clauses, and asides, mocking the faddish theorizing that bedevils modern archaeology.

"I don't know what we would have done if we'd had to devise a *paradigm*." He spat out the word like something nasty in the tea. "Anyone who approaches the past with his mind made up will find exactly what he expects to find. As somebody once said, each generation gets the Stonehenge it deserves."

Despite his disdain for theory, Pendergast did not decide to dig at Lamanai from mere curiosity. He had good reasons for thinking that the site might shed light on one of the great mysteries in New World archaeology: the apparently spontaneous collapse of Classic Maya civilization (A.D. 250-900) during the ninth and tenth centuries. At that time most cities in the lowlands of Guatemala and Belize were abandoned; Palenque, Tikal, Yaxchilán, and many others were reclaimed by the patient forest. It was clear from the size of Lamanai's pyramids that much of the city dated from the Classic period, but there was also evidence that Lamanai had struggled on. When the Spaniards reached this corner of Belize in the mid-sixteenth century, they built a mission here, whose remains the British would later call Indian Church. "Obviously there must have been Mayas still living at Lamanai," Pendergast said. "No religious order, no matter how dedicated or fanatic, builds its church where there are no parishioners."

Pendergast's work in Belize has made him a local folk hero. At Altun Ha he made one of the most spectacular Maya discoveries of recent times. Unlike Egyptian pyramids, Maya ones were primarily temple platforms, not tombs. But behind the staircase ascending the main Altun Ha structure, he uncovered a burial chamber containing a priest of the sun. Next to the skeleton, amid fine pottery and the remains of wooden artifacts and bolts of cloth, lay a head of Kinich Ahau, the sun god, carved from a single piece of jade. The ten-pound stone, beautifully worked and polished, is about the size of a human head, but to modern eyes its features are grotesque: iconography dictated that the sun god be cross-eyed, with a fanged mouth, a fat nose, and large cauliflower ears. Carved in the sixth century and insured in the twentieth for several million dollars, Kinich Ahau has become Belize's equivalent of the crown jewels.

Archaeologists call the region now occupied by Mexico, Guatemala, Belize, and parts of Honduras and El Salvador "Mesoamerica"—a term reflecting the cultural integrity of the area in which the Olmec, Maya, Teotihuacan, Toltec, and Aztec civilizations arose. The various ancient peoples of Mesoamerica influenced one another much as did the Egyptians, Greeks, and Romans of the Mediterranean basin. Between about 7000 and 3000 B.C., early Mesoamericans domesticated turkeys and dogs and invented agriculture. With farming came settled villages, population growth, organized religion, and social hierarchy—culminating in societies of great complexity and sophistication.

About 1500 B.C., the Olmecs of the Mexican gulf coast established Mesoamerica's first full-blown civilization, and it seems they influenced the rapidly developing Maya to the east. By 500 B.C., the Olmecs were on the wane and the Maya were coming into their own. The following seven centuries—those roughly coeval with the rise, apogee, and decline of Rome—are known as the late Pre-Classic period. It was the age when the Maya evolved their mathematics, writing, astronomy, and architecture—arts that flowered dramatically in the succeeding Classic period, which also lasted about seven centuries.

While Europe slipped into the Dark Ages, Maya astronomers were making highly accurate measurements of the solar year, the lunar month, and the apparent revolutions of the planets. They predicted eclipses, calculated planetary conjunctions (important in their astrology), and constructed a great calendar that was nothing less than a theoretical model of the universe based on the measurement of time. As recently as the last century, European intellectuals thought that the whole of creation was only a few thousand years old (a belief still held by 47 per cent of Americans, according to a Gallup poll). The Maya guessed that time is infinite. Their hieroglyphic inscriptions are filled with dates revealing that they ran their calculations backwards and forwards over an immense temporal landscape, pinpointing sacred events millions, even billions, of years in the past and future.

All this was done with elegantly simple methods. Classic Maya technology was in the Stone Age; they had no metal tools, no telescopes or clocks. What they did have was an advanced arithmetic with place notation and the concept of zero—ideas unknown to the Greeks, Romans, and mediaeval Europe until long after the great Maya cities were in ruins. The Maya calendar was based not on years but on days, the most stable measure of earthly time. By watching heavenly bodies over centuries, perhaps millennia, through apertures in temples and towers, Maya astronomers were able to refine their naked-eye sightings until errors became extremely small. Only fragments of their ancient knowledge have come down to us in stone inscriptions and four surviving pre-Columbian books, but enough is known to show that a Maya calculation for the synodical period of Venus differed by only fourteen seconds *per year* from the figure determined by atomic clocks.

Most of Lamanai is still covered by high jungle. Huge trees rise from buttress roots, gripping the piles of rubble like giant octopi.

The forest floor is surprisingly open, carpeted in leaves, dotted with philodendrons. It is gloomy, restful; the air smells like a compost heap; only narrow shafts of sunlight pierce the jungle canopy, a thick pelt of foliage beginning fifty feet above the ground. In the dry season there are few mosquitoes, but one has to watch out for "doctor flies", sinister practitioners who inject their victims with a local anaesthetic while taking a hefty blood sample.

The archaeologists' first work was cutting trails and mapping the city on a surveyed grid. They found visible stone ruins in a strip more than two miles long and a third of a mile wide on a low ridge along the lakeshore. The student crew soon dubbed the larger mounds and platforms Lag, Holiday House, Fut, Ottawa, and other irreverent names that fall from the tongue more readily than grid designations.

The structure known as Lag is the tallest at Lamanai. A trail opens in a tiny clearing, and there it is—a great staircase climbing 112 feet out of the jungle. The steps are in good condition at the bottom, but they are large even for gringo legs, and certainly for the stocky Maya.

"I don't think the priests climbed up in a hurry," Pendergast remarked during a tour of the site on our first morning. "These stairs were really an elevated stage for long, slow ceremonies as the officiants made their dignified way to the top."

What rites were performed here? Who or what was worshipped? Maya religion was as baroque as Hinduism or Catholicism; it is an oversimplification to speak of a sun god, a moon goddess, a maize god, and so forth. Quetzalcoatl, the Aztecs' Feathered Serpent, patron of learning and medicine, was worshipped by the Maya under other names; they also revered a form of Tezcatlipoca, the Smoking Mirror, aptly linked with politics and royalty. Human sacrifice was less common among the Maya than the Aztecs, but beneath the finest carved monument at

Lamanai—a stela, or upright slab, with a hieroglyphic inscription and a relief of the city's ruler in full fig—Pendergast found the bones of half a dozen children.

Lag's summit pokes like an island from the forest canopy. We looked out over the lagoon, the glinting swamps to the east, the tall trees—mahoganies, silkcottons, and *guanacastes*—standing above tufted palms. From below came liquid bird calls, the croaking of frogs, and a sudden crack when a termite-weakened limb gave way.

To find out when the city began, when people first settled in this area, Pendergast took cores of lagoon sediment and examined the ancient pollen. Maize—a sure sign of farming—appeared in force in 1500 B.C. The earliest buildings he has found date from about 800 B.C. Lag had reached its present height by 100 B.C., when it may have been one of the largest Maya buildings anywhere. Like most of Mesoamerica's stepped pyramids, it was built up over centuries, as the Maya added layer after layer of masonry to the original temple mound. The overgrown pile of rubble that greeted Pendergast eleven years ago turned out to have several previous incarnations well preserved within it. By the time of Lamanai's heyday, the early corn farmers' humble village had grown into a city of 20,000, perhaps 50,000, people. Society had stratified into classes and trades, the powerful living in stone palaces beside plazas and temples, the artisans surrounding them in suburbs, and the thatched huts of the peasantry stretching across many square miles of kitchen gardens and fields.

We descended into the jungle and after a hundred yards or so came to the middle of the plaza over which Lag presided. The woods were still, almost as dark as twilight, the only sound a whine of insects dancing in meagre sunbeams. Suddenly there came heavy breaths, impossibly loud, like Darth Vader having an asthma attack. The sound rose to a frantic snoring, then broke into roars and barks. "Howler monkeys," said Pendergast.

They were up in a tree with a trunk six feet thick and a leafless crown spreading eighty feet above us. I could see three large animals, as big as baboons, with long panther-like tails curled gracefully around the branches. They were eating a pendulous fruit known in Belize as horse's balls. Alan shot yards of film, a red hairy face looking up, three black hairy faces looking down. When the monkeys had had enough of us, they started throwing turds.

We moved on to a narrow court between terraced platforms, where ancient athletes played the ritual game of Mesoamerica. Two teams contested a heavy ball of solid rubber, and to make things more interesting, they were not allowed to touch the ball with hands or feet. The game represented the eternal struggle between night and day, and was also a way to vent political disputes. Nobles bet heavily on high-stakes matches between rival towns. Unlike the Incas of Peru, the Maya were not empire builders. They were the Greeks of the New World, living in small city states that competed in sport, art, and astronomy, and waged sporadic, inconclusive wars.

Pendergast pointed out a large stone disk marking the centre of the court. Here he had found a strange offering of several pots. Their style dated them to the beginning of the tenth century—significant because it meant that Lamanai was still building ball courts while most other Maya cities were being abandoned. But this did not surprise him nearly as much as what was in one of the bowls: a pool of mercury, something never before encountered in a Maya site. "No paradigm," he said, "could have predicted that."

It was almost noon and getting hot, even in deep shade. Pendergast started along another trail leading to camp and lunch. We were all sweaty and tired, but he kept talking. "Every season I think I'm beginning to understand this place, and then something completely new and unexpected opens up. I'll give you another example of a little mystery. In the southern part of the site we found a burial. There's a man and a woman and a tiny baby, possibly a fetus or a stillborn. They were sitting in a pit side by side, and the woman had her arm around the man's shoulders. You can almost see something of these people, but you can't answer any of the basic questions about them. Were they married? Is the child theirs? Why are they there? What killed them? The range of answers is almost beyond calculation." He paused and mopped his face with a spotted handkerchief, as if exhausted by the thought. "You're on the other side of a huge barrier. Sometimes, you get to the point where you feel you can't say anything at all. If you just stick a shovel in the ground and then go off and write the definitive prehistory, you might as well shred it and spread it on your rhododendrons, because it'll make the blooms a lot bigger."

It took me several days to learn my way around the network of leafy tunnels linking Lamanai's main buildings. One afternoon I emerged unexpectedly in "Ottawa", a residential complex where the elite had lived. Ottawa's inhabitants evidently had a mania for modification, renovation, and senseless rebuilding—phenomena only too familiar at its modern namesake.

"I've examined garbage dumps from the upper-class neighbourhoods here and at Altun Ha," Pendergast told me over a beer that evening. "And there's no doubt these people lived off the fat of the land. They ate a lot of venison and turtle."

Archaeologists are still puzzling over reasons for the Maya collapse. Theories of plague, soil exhaustion, social upheaval, and climate change have been advanced, but it would be naïve to opt for just one of them. The fall of a civilization is likely to be a complex affair. Like others before and since, the Maya gradually created problems for themselves that became increasingly difficult to solve. Their skeletons reveal that body size declined throughout the Classic period, suggesting that nutrition levels fell as the population grew. Even more telling are differences between upper- and lower-class bones. Nobles, priests, and bureaucrats were robust, often fat; workers and peasants became stunted with passing generations. It seems that the Maya elite came to hold the currently fashionable view that the rich must be allowed to get richer, while the poor need the threat of hunger to keep them from idleness. If this attitude led to revolution, then one can only reflect how history repeats itself in Central America.

Recent satellite photographs show that the swampy parts of the Maya lowlands were crisscrossed with canals dividing raised fields for intensive cultivation, which explains how large cities thrived in a rainforest. But perhaps the Classic Maya, like many peoples around the world today, eventually disrupted the ecosystem to the point where it could no longer support them.

Pendergast wanted to do more work in the ancient farmland west of Holiday House but was thwarted by modern farmers making new use of the old fields. Lamanai has been invaded by squatters fleeing the wars in El Salvador and Guatemala. Some of them are producing a cash crop suited to remote locations. "There are just too many characters out there growing Mexican laughing tobacco. One day, three of them popped out of the trees and pointed submachine guns at us. All they said was *No.* So we stick to the ruins."

On my last morning at Lamanai, I set off with Pendergast at 6.30 to visit the south end of the site, where his crew were working. A sheet of mist was lifting from the lake into the trees; the water was platinum and still. Once, a brief uproar from the bush shattered the silence, a noise like a hacksaw ripping sheets of tin. "Now you've heard a chachalaca," he said. "They're weird-looking birds no bigger than a chicken. That was *one.* A whole flock will destroy your mind."

We came to the squatter village, a collection of shacks made of corrugated iron, cracked planks, palmetto poles, and tarred cardboard, on the far side of a patch of forest that serves as an informal boundary between it and the archaeologists' camp. Though illegal because it sits on land reserved for antiquities, the village has elected a "mayor". Claude Bélanger and three Maya workers were digging in the mayor's front garden—the man had built on an ancient house, and they were excavating it to make a point. A grinding stone stood exposed in a corner of what was once the kitchen, and you could see that the white floors were decorated with red trim where they met the walls. Obviously this house had been far superior to the mayor's, even though the mayor does have a colour TV.

These remains date from the Post-Classic period, which spans the six hundred years from the great collapse to the arrival of the Spaniards in the sixteenth century. Somehow Lamanai carried on through these years, albeit in reduced circumstances. "Possibly the lagoon provided a secure food supply when there was famine elsewhere," Pendergast suggested. "Or if the main problems were political, then the fact that Lamanai was a minor centre at the end of the Classic may have been an advantage." He found that from about 900 to 1200, the inhabitants continued to repair the fronts of the old pyramids, even though they began dumping garbage at the backs and sides. By the time the Spanish came, the great temples of the past had been left to the jungle, and the religious life of the city had shifted to small shrines here in the southern district, where most of the people were living.

The Spanish built their Lamanai mission sometime before 1582, and the city was mentioned again in the records when two friars visited the faithful in 1618. But when one of them came back in 1641, he found that the Maya had taken up arms, burned down the church, and, as he put it, "returned to the vomit of the idolatries and abominations of their ancestors." The mission walls that stand today are from the second of two early churches built next to each other. All that remains of the first is a low mound. When Pendergast excavated this he discovered that the Spanish foundations enclosed the base of a small Maya temple. And when he dug at the second church, he found offerings of Maya figurines and a stela set upright in front of the sanctuary.

The sequence of events from about 1450 to 1650 suddenly became clear. There had been a Maya town with at least one of its important shrines in use when Europeans arrived. The Spanish priests, as they did in many places, pulled down the temple and built their church on the very site of the worship they hoped to uproot. For a while they prospered, even building a larger church next door. But then the Maya rebelled, burned the church, and apparently rededicated its ruins to the old gods of Lamanai. At the back wall of the sanctuary, right behind where the Christian altar had stood, Pendergast found a ceramic crocodile with gaping jaws at either end. The wheel had come full circle.

The British established control over Belize about 1800. They brought in African slaves to cut mahogany, and Chinese coolies to work some ill-fated sugar plantations—one at Lamanai. By that time the Maya, like all native Americans, had been severely reduced by smallpox and other Old World diseases, but it is possible that a remnant group still lived at "Indian Church". As in North America, the British wanted the land, not its people; several times during the nineteenth century they drove the Belize Maya into Guatemala and Yucatán. One old man who recently returned to Lamanai still remembers when a logging company's bulldozers destroyed his village here in the early 1900s. Apart from the squatters and Pendergast's crew, that old man's people may well have been the last of the ancient city's inhabitants, the last ciphers on a population graph that seems to have fallen steadily from the ninth century to the present.

The British sugar mill lasted a decade, the Spanish mission half a century, the Maya city of Lamanai more than 3,000 years. If Europeans had not invaded America, the Maya might eventually have rebuilt their civilization. About five million people, mostly in

Guatemala and Yucatán, still speak Maya languages and preserve many traditions, including knowledge of the ancient calendar. Today, depending on where they live, they face violent repression, forced assimilation, and rapid development.

The future of Lamanai itself is equally uncertain, threatened by problems that pervade Central America and reach far beyond it. Archaeology is too often a race between the professionals and the looters. While collectors in New York, London, or Paris have millions to spend on Maya treasures, the dispossessed of Central America must rob their past to survive. It is the familiar predicament of poor countries with rich pasts.

If the worst happens, and Lamanai is pillaged, David Pendergast's work will not have been in vain. He has at least created a scientific record of what was there, and when that record is fully analysed and published, we will have a profile of a city that weathered the fall of the Classic Maya world more than a thousand years ago. As the results from Lamanai are compared with those from other sites, the portrait of a civilization disintegrating under stress will gradually emerge. And perhaps in that reflection from a distant place and time, we may see something more clearly of ourselves.

FOUR

A Jungle Michelangelo

The Belize trip rescued me from the horse latitudes in which I'd been drifting with the last chapter of *On Fiji Islands.* I came home with a fresh eye and new energy to finish the book. I moved out of the tower block and found a house on the edge of the city. There were bikers next door—they looked like close cousins of the Grim Reapers with whom I'd once shared a tenement back in Calgary—but at least there were also trees and grass.

Lamanai had rekindled my interest in the Maya, whose ancient civilization I'd studied briefly at university. During the next winter, I made a three-month journey through Belize, Guatemala, and Mexico, gathering material for what became *Time Among the Maya.*

Travel writing was enjoying a new vogue, thanks largely to Bruce Chatwin's *In Patagonia* and Paul Theroux's *Great Railway Bazaar*. Even Canada's sedate monthly, *Saturday Night*, which turned one hundred in 1987, caught the wave. George Galt, *Saturday Night*'s new literary editor, put the word out that travel pieces would again be welcome (they hadn't been for some years). I knew George from his own travel books, among them a delightful memoir of the Aegean Islands, and *Whistlestop*, a wry yet amiable train journey across Canada from sea to sea. We had lunch one day near the magazine's office in Toronto's high-rise core. I was the only man in the restaurant without a tie. George, who favoured plaid shirts and woollen ties, was gentlemanly but hardly "downtown". What he was looking for, he said, were "non-fiction short stories". I've never heard a better definition of what a travel piece should be.

I'd finished a draft of *Time Among the Maya* by then, and "A Jungle Michelangelo" grew from a chapter of the manuscript. The passage opens in Palenque—the modern town near the famous ruins of that name in southern Mexico.

THE MAN IN THE HAT is drinking rum and Coke and leaning across the bar towards the barmaid, a pretty American blonde. He's wearing khaki and a wide-brimmed brown fedora. He looks about fifty—grey hair and a red, boyish face. I hear him saying:

"How does a girl like you manage to stay single?"

"I'm not."

"Who's the lucky guy, then?" She smiles and polishes a glass.

I introduce myself. "Len," he says. "Glad to meet you. So you're from Canada, eh? So am I, and here we are in the Canada Hotel, isn't that something?"

"It's *Cañada*, actually. It means ravine," the barmaid says.

"Oh, is that right?" Len takes off his hat and scratches a sunburnt bald spot. I buy him another Cuba Libre and get a beer for myself.

"I hear you're thinking of going to Bonampak and Yaxchilán. Perhaps we could join up?" I suggest. I've been looking for a way to get to these remote ruins in the jungle. They lie near the Guatemalan border, in the territory of the Lacandón, a small group of forest Maya who escaped the conquering Spaniards and are only now abandoning their ancient religion for fundamentalist Christianity.

"Let me tell you what I'm doin' here," Len says. "I'm not a tourist, see. Concrete's my business, and I'm down here for a week collecting samples. I study ancient concretes. I make my living with the modern ones, but the old ones get me out around the world. Now these ruins you're talkin' about, are they Mayan ruins like the ones here?"

It isn't difficult to persuade him, especially when he hears I'm "not a tourist" either. He has a rented Volkswagen beetle and a tent, but no Spanish; could I contribute half the car costs, some food, and translation? It's a deal.

"You won't mind if we stop along the road for snakes, will you?" he adds. "I'm a bit of a herpetologist, see."

"Oh, do you know the species around here? I'd like to learn."

"Well, not exactly. Last time in Mexico I got this snake rather like a king snake. It was brown. When I was in the Amazon I got a *beautiful* boa constrictor! Someone had run him over but the skin was perfect. I got him all skinned and salted and smuggled back into Canada. Laid it out in my basement—almost fifteen feet long it was—and my darn dogs ate it."

We leave soon after dawn the next day. "You drive," Len says. "You know, I race powerboats and fast cars, but I don't like to drive down here. Prefer to watch for snakes." He settles back into the passenger seat. Then: "What! No hat?"

I explain that my cotton sun hat, bought in Egypt from a man wearing a pile of them, had got so stained and torn that I threw it away.

"The older they get the better I like 'em. But the wife, she threw my old one out. I bought this new for the trip." He takes off his fedora and shows me the label inside. "It's the genuine Indiana Jones model, see?"

Good pavement soon gives way to broken asphalt—much worse than no paving at all—followed after ten miles or so by gravel. The hills and valleys have been devastated by development. Farming, ranching, and logging have conspired to murder the jungle. The fragments of forest that remain look like green rags on a corpse.

"The *jungle* begins at Chancalá!" Len says, consulting a sketch map he made last night (jungle is one of his favourite words). "That's what the fella at the Canada told me." But after Chancalá, twenty-five miles from Palenque, the country is almost as threadbare as before. The road gets worse, deeply rippled and rutted by heavy trucks. Like Len, I've always imagined the Mexican side of the Petén jungle, known as the *selva lacandona*, as a virgin forest of giant trees. But what we see resembles something from the American west of the 1930s: a very wide, very bad road down which vehicles approach in a strange sidewinding minuet, trailing boas of dust as they weave between potholes and stones. White powder covers grass and bushes and endless barbed wire. Every few miles we come to big ranch buildings. Between the *ranchos* are *ranchitos*, the tin and plank shacks of migrants from other parts of Mexico. These people now outnumber the Lacandón a hundred to one. Nueva Coahuila, Nuevo Guerrero—the names recall the dustiest, most hopeless parts of the Mexican republic. Men in cowboy hats and leather boots drink beer in roadside bars; *ranchero* music lopes through the burning air; women with loads on their heads shuffle along the roadside, their cheap gingham dresses as faded as the land at midday; only those new to puberty look young. At such places the musk of the tropics is swamped by gasoline, alcohol, urine, and human shit. Huge logs lie in ditches, fading with neglect.

At last the road begins to wind upwards into heaving limestone hills. This land is poor for farming, but even here wildfires started by colonists have left acres of blackened skeletons like the blasted woods of the Somme. Slowly new growth is creeping back, and it seems to gain strength as we gain height. Here and there the dark green foliage is relieved by yellow myrtle and purple wigs of morning glory. The road gets narrower; trees begin to touch above it. This forest was felled once before, by the ancient Maya, and it returned. Perhaps, after a thousand years, it can survive another assault; but such a cycle offers little for those dependent on its fragile bounty.

We pass a turning for New Palestine, a name redolent of missionary fundamentalism. About eighty miles from Palenque—and maybe only twenty from the Guatemalan border—we come to another turning and a shack. Lacandón youngsters run out, brandishing strings of beads and toy bows. With their cotton smocks and wild hair they look like Victorian slum children dressed for bed. They crowd around, shouting prices and shoving trinkets in our faces. It's impossible to ask directions. I drive on a few hundred yards to a forestry department office, but it's empty and the children run until they catch up with the car. Len purchases some respite with a string of beads. I suppose it had to happen: the natives forcing beads on the explorers. At last an adult confirms that this is the fork for Bonampak.

Before long we come to some outlying huts belonging to the Lacandón village of Lacanhá. A young man sells us warm Cokes. We take his advice to park the car here and walk the last six miles.

At first the trail is easy. One might be tempted to try it with a car, but after about a mile there's a streambed spanned by a makeshift bridge of tree trunks—only a vehicle with a winch would get across that. We advance in a tortoise-and-hare motion. Len likes to hike slowly and steadily; I prefer to march ahead and rest until he catches up. (The Maya have a version of this myth: eclipses are contests between a turtle sun and rabbit moon.) After an hour I sit down on a log and watch a procession of leafcutter ants waving chips of greenery aloft like battle standards.

Two hours pass and there's still no sign of the ruins. The sun was high when we began, striking down on our heads from between the trees, but now we have shade and can appreciate the wildlife: parrots, morpho butterflies the colour of sky in a stained-glass window, and the inevitable circling, ever-hopeful *zopilote.* Len glares at the vulture.

"I wonder if he knows something we don't know. Six miles is a long way. You know, when you said six miles I thought, I drive that far every day into town and it's nothin', but on foot in this climate it's another matter." He drops his pack, uncorks his canteen, and peers anxiously inside. "We'd better watch our water. Boy, if we run out of water, we're sunk."

After two and a half hours comes a smell of woodsmoke. Twenty minutes later the trail ends in a clearing of mown grass. There are three or four thatched huts, an old truck on blocks, a couple of wooden bungalows. A young man stripped to the waist is washing at a tap. He's Mauricio, an epigrapher from INAH (the Mexican anthropological institute), working on conservation of the famous murals. An elderly man emerges from one of the huts and gazes proprietorially in my direction.

"You'd better have a word with that gentleman there," Mauricio says. "He's one of the site guardians." Len arrives, panting; the guardian agrees to let us camp the night, but he isn't sure we can see the ruins today: it's already four o'clock and the men have knocked off. Other employees appear. One agrees to show us round the site provided we pay him "overtime". There's an air of suspicion and resentment of visitors—justified, no doubt, because of looters, but rather crushing after such a long walk. Len produces a letter given him by a Mexican archaeologist for whom he took samples on an earlier trip. Eventually we convince them we're *gente de confianza*, trustworthy folk.

Local Maya don't seem to be employed here, even though it was a Lacandón, Chan Bor, who first led an outsider, Giles Healey, to the ruins in 1946. Healey claimed that the Lacandón didn't know the frescoes existed, which seems highly unlikely. But it's hard to resist his story that as he entered the painted rooms a black puma strolled out.

You walk down a wide path shaded by colossal buttressed trees to a plaza; on the far side is a steep hill artfully terraced to form a pyramid. Broad steps climb to a row of shrines. Dark doorways stare like a gap-toothed mouth beneath a tall brow of rock and exuberant vegetation. The buildings on the plaza are piles of rubble except for a small three-roomed palace containing the only complete set of Maya wall paintings from the Classic period. The odds against their survival are incalculable. First, that they should be here at all: Bonampak was a small centre, relatively unimportant, overshadowed by Yaxchilán twenty miles away on the Usumacinta River. Second, that the paintings should be of such quality: far from being provincial, these rank with the finest representational work that has come down to us in any medium used by the ancient Maya. It is as if Michelangelo had chosen to paint the ceiling of a country church instead of the Sistine Chapel. Somehow these masterpieces behind unguarded doors survived the iconoclasm that ravaged several cities at the time of the collapse. Somehow the invading jungle, which levelled every other structure at Bonampak except the shrines on the hill, spared this building. And by a happy accident, eleven centuries of rain seeping through the mortar of the vault precipitated a thin layer of limestone that sealed the murals against the smoke of Lacandón incense and the atmosphere.

Since 1946 the murals have not been so lucky. Conservation and study were hampered by political disputes. Visitors were in the habit of throwing water or kerosene on the paintings to bring out the colours. Now the Mexicans have begun major restoration. The building wears a hat of corrugated iron, and electric fans stir the damp air inside. Our guide removes screens from the doors (put there to keep out bats) and shows us in.

"Absolutely no photographs."

"Even without flash?" asks Len, who has fast film.

"Even without flash."

There's little point in taking pictures with all the scaffolding and paraphernalia anyway. In the first room conservation is well advanced. The stalactite coating has been scraped back in neat strips, revealing faces, hands, bright colours, and calligraphy. I've seen a replica of this building in Mexico City and am expecting to be disappointed by the real thing. But within moments I no longer notice the clutter and whirring fans. The paintings are able to dominate such intrusions. Immediately I feel that ineffable tingle famous things can bestow when one is in their presence for the first time. I felt it in the burial chambers of Egyptian pyramids (though not outside), and again in the Qorikancha, or "Sun Temple", of the Incas; I felt it in front of Bosch's paintings in Madrid. It comes from proximity to something ancient, alien; from being in a space filled with dead voices and the silent echo of the years.

In the first room, on the triangular west wall, the ruling family—the lord, his wife, and another woman—are sitting elegantly on a stone dais. The focus of everyone's attention is a royal child, presumably the heir apparent, held up before the crowd. Below, on the walls beneath the spring of the vault, a musical procession entertains the lords. Some of the musicians are human, wearing breechclouts and elaborate cotton turbans; others are masked as grotesque supernatural beings of both earth and sea. A manikin with a vegetal head and the T sign of the wind in his eye is presenting an ear of corn to another. Above them on the right rears a character from Pincher Martin's death-dream, snapping lobster claws in place of arms. At his feet sits a man with a crocodile head.

This fantasia contrasts with the scene above the door, where the lord of Bonampak is dressing for a great occasion. He is backed by an arc of quetzal plumes, while longer tailfeathers of the same bird erupt in a spray from the starched cotton of his headdress, which itself includes fish, bird, and reptile motifs. His head is in profile; an enormous jade spool hides his left ear, and a jade collar covers his shoulders and chest like mail. His torso is bare to the waist, below which he wears a jaguar kilt. All this splendour might be overwhelming were it not for informal touches. A manservant or minor lord is adjusting the jade cuff at the ruler's wrist, attentive as any gentleman's gentleman. A noble standing behind has his arm outstretched and his mouth open in speech. He is about to tug the servant's hair and say, *Just a minute, you.* Other attendants are fussing nervously. *Is everything all right? What have you done with the jades? Let me check that jaguar skin.*

The concluding ceremonies are shown in the third room, to the west. Members of the ruling family appear again: four matronly women sitting on a dais, engaged in the Maya sacrifice of shedding blood from their tongues onto paper sheets. But the rite doesn't stop them having a lively conversation. Another woman sits cross-legged on the floor with a toddler in her arms, and she is talking over her shoulder to one of those above. Like their modern descendants, these ancient Maya seem relaxed during religious rituals. The scene is personal, even private.

It is the central room that gives meaning to the whole narrative, and nothing could be further from the touching glimpses of family and womanhood. As you enter, you walk into a battle that covers every wall but the one at your back. Grimacing faces are surmounted by heraldic crests and feathered helms. Men clothed in jaguar-skin tunics and gaiters are leaping, dodging, grasping enemies by the hair, plunging obsidian-tipped lances through chests. The enemy, an abject group of half-naked barbarians, cringe and die. Realism is achieved by comic-book techniques.

The figures are outlined in black and filled with washes of strong colour: copper for the skin of the victors, brown for that of the enemy; green for the feathers, yellow with black spots for jaguar pelts. Great attention is paid to the cast of an eye, the pout of lips, the jut of a jaw. The fighters are as mobile as athletes caught in action by a camera. Depth is achieved through bold superimposition and foreshortening. The fetor of the small room becomes the sweat of battle, the reek of intestines spilled in the steaming forest. Aided by distant parrots and a woodpecker's tattoo, you hear the battle cries, the crash of wood and stone and bone.

The entire room is propaganda of the most blatant and effective kind. White caption-boxes filled with hieroglyphs tell the story. Bonampak's troops could be officers of the Reich, and their quarry some despicable non-Aryan breed. But both sides look distinctly Maya. Who is being attacked? Is this an example of a raid to capture sacrificial victims? Or is it, as the faded writing seems to say, a major offensive by the allied forces of Yaxchilán and Bonampak against a rival? The lord and lady shown are Chaan Muan, who came to power in 776, and his wife, Lady Rabbit, a Yaxchilán princess. Most of Bonampak's monuments date from Chaan Muan's reign, suggesting that the city enjoyed a brief rise to prominence before the collapse of Classic Maya civilization in the following century.

The battle's aftermath is painted above the door. Humbled captives plead for their lives. To modern eyes there is a gloating cruelty in the scene. Chaan Muan—so lifelike that you recognize his face from previous appearances—stands regally clasping a lance encased with jaguar skin. On either side of him other notables parade in elaborate cloaks and huge animal-head crests, the brilliant colours of these figures standing out against a blue background. The scene takes place on tiers of red-painted steps, probably the very flight that climbs the hill from the plaza. The butt of the lord's spear rests behind the forehead of a dead captive sprawled backwards across three steps, in a pose that might indeed have come from the brush of Michelangelo—little in Europe can compare with the draftsmanship of this figure until the Renaissance. Nearby are three terrified survivors with blood dripping from their fingernails, and at the sprawled figure's foot rests a head on a bed of leaves, an oddly peaceful smile still playing at its lips.

The triumph celebrated on these walls was a brief one. The dates on this building were the last the city inscribed. The murals were never quite finished; caption-boxes were left unfilled. As Mary Miller wrote in her study of the frescoes: "The story of Bonampak ends. The little heir probably never reached the throne. The site was abandoned; the artists were dispersed. Painting of this calibre vanished from ancient Mesoamerica."

I remember a Gahan Wilson cartoon I saw some years ago in *Playboy*. It showed a city devastated by atomic bombs; a loudspeaker hung from wires among the ruins, mechanically repeating a victory announcement that ended with the refrain *This is a recorded message.*

When we come out, the sun is hovering above the trees to the west. Shrines on the hill are outlined in gold, but the wall of rock and vegetation behind is deeply shadowed. A great carved stela in the middle of the plaza—among the largest ever erected by the Maya—is thrown into sharp relief. Scaffolding surrounds it at the moment, but the fierce eye of Chaan Muan is still able to transfix. I ask our guide if any Lacandón come here with offerings.

"Not for the last few years."

"Why not?"

"Because the young people are either evangelicals or out of hand." We retrieve our packs and pitch the tent beside the INAH camp. After a foul supper of cold tinned frankfurters, Len produces his rum. He talks about earlier trips: how he got lost in the

Amazon near Manaus, eaten by bedbugs in Iraq, stricken by a strange lung disease in Egypt after stealing a mummy's leg.

There's no moon and no cloud; by eight o'clock the sky is obsidian speckled with the Milky Way's luminous dust. I lie on my back and watch shooting stars, which the Maya believed were cigar butts thrown down by the gods.

FIVE

The Death-List People

There is of course a dark side to Central America, especially to the story of the Maya. At Lamanai I had seen a squatter camp beside the ancient ruins, and many of those squatters were refugees who had fled the terrible war in Guatemala. In *Time Among the Maya* I did not write only about the Maya past; equally important in the book were the five or six million living Maya who struggle to survive as a people, to continue in modern form the brilliant culture of their ancestors. In Guatemala these people and others are the victims of oppression, injustice, and violence as bad as, or worse than, the more familiar horrors of South Africa, El Salvador, and Cambodia. Guatemala always eludes the world's front pages; it continues to do so, even though a Quiché Maya, Rigoberta Menchú, won the 1992 Nobel Peace Prize.

"The Death-List People" is about Guatemala's civil war and the victims who fled their country for haven in Canada. Since I wrote the article in the winter of 1986, the Soviet bloc has disintegrated, the Reagan era has ended, and South Africa has begun serious reform. But comparable change has yet to take root in Guatemala. Those cynical about Vinicio Cerezo's presidency (1986-1991) were proved right. His successor, Jorge Serrano, appeared equally in thrall to the generals. The most encouraging developments have been the replacement of Serrano by the respected human rights ombudsman, Ramiro de León, in June 1993, and the return of refugees—most of them Mayas—from camps in Mexico. The first group went back early in 1993, and the rest are being urged by Mexico to follow soon. But already there have been disturbing signs of army activity in the places they are reoccupying. I hope the world will at last find time for Guatemala, and watch their progress carefully.

IN THE SMART FOREST HILL apartment he shares with his Canadian benefactor, a man shows me a list of names beneath a proclamation bearing a crudely drawn logo, a wedge shattering a hammer and sickle. The heading (in Spanish) reads: Secret Anti-Communist Army, Bulletin No. 6. His name is there, together with other "cowards and bad Guatemalans judged and condemned by the Supreme Tribunal of the *Ejército Secreto Anticomunista*." He asks me not to reveal his identity, so I shall call him Eduardo Martínez.

"The secret police checked my family after I left. If they see my name in print they might do something to make me shut up. Not to me, of course, but to someone close to me in Guatemala." He's only in his mid-thirties, but there's a weight of experience in his voice, his shoulders, the lines on his dark face. He goes to the kitchen and comes back with a cigarette that trembles in his hand. Ash falls onto his white cotton shirt embroidered with quetzal birds, Guatemala's national emblem and a symbol of freedom. The quetzal is nearly extinct.

"Guatemalan embassies collect clippings," he adds, "and the

military police back home have the very latest computer equipment."

Martínez is alone in Canada. He hasn't seen his wife and children since he fled eight years ago, and in that time the marriage has broken down. In Guatemala he was a qualified electrician. Now he works in a laundry and spends much of his free time giving talks on the situation in his homeland. "My country," he says in a parody of patriotism, "is one of the few countries in the world where you won't find any political prisoners. That's how bad the repression is." A grimace agitates his goatee, sad humour flickers in his eyes. Guatemala is full of sinister jokes, some intentional, others not. I found it hard, when I was there, to tell them apart. I wondered if anyone saw the irony in the cut-out policemen that halt traffic at road works. Cardboard cops in a police state! Was anyone offended by the ubiquitous advertisements for pantyhose in a country where half the people have no shoes? You couldn't even buy a Coke with a clear conscience: the Coca-Cola workers' union had been culled by death squads, and the survivors circulated leaflets saying *This product contains human blood.*

It was union activity (at a different multinational company) that led to Martínez's exile early in 1979. "The company would not respect the terms of the collective agreement they'd signed with us. We met with the president of the company, who was a European. We went to the Ministry of Labour. They held an investigation and found that the workers were not at fault."

When legal procedures failed, other methods were tried. Martínez, as general secretary, was offered a bribe to stop making trouble. He turned it down. "After that, a high-ranking police officer came to the factory with a dozen armed men in plainclothes. The company president said he wanted the union smashed. The policeman said, 'Don't tell me stories—just tell me who we're going to kill. What I need is names.' We heard about this conversation from a contact in the government who later fled to Panama." Soon afterwards the Secret Anti-Communist Army death list came out. A few weeks later, two carloads of gunmen tried to kidnap Martínez in Guatemala City. He fled to Costa Rica.

"Even there I didn't feel safe. There are Guatemalan agents in all neighbouring countries. I had a lot of psychological problems. Every time I saw a Toyota jeep—the kind our police use—I would freeze. I began talking to myself. I'd heard that Canada accepted refugees, so with the money I had left I flew to Toronto and asked for asylum at the airport."

For political refugees, arriving in Canada is neither an end nor a new beginning, but an initiation into limbo: first a bureaucratic limbo while the refugee's case is considered; then the limbo of separation from culture, friends, and relatives; a truncated career; an interrupted life. The exile, unlike the immigrant, looks back to what he has left, not forwards to a new life. To stop looking back is to betray those who stayed behind, whether alive, dead, or "disappeared". (Guatemalans claim that "disappear" was first used as a transitive verb in their country, with the debut of organized death squads in the 1960s.) Martínez was one of the first to come from Guatemala and there were few structures in place to deal with him. Immigration officials took away his passport and put him in a hotel near Toronto airport. For two days he stayed there with no news. Then came a hearing to see whether he merited refugee status. "It was like a small court. I had to prove that my life was in danger, and that I hadn't come to Canada for economic reasons. I showed them the death list with my name on it. They let me stay but they imposed conditions. I wasn't allowed to attend any school or college—not even to learn English. I couldn't be hired by an employer without ministry approval."

The ban on learning English was official policy at that time. Refugees suspect it was intended to prevent them from gaining a foothold in Canada while their cases were under consideration.

Members of the Inter-Church Committee on Human Rights in Latin America (an organization formed by the Canadian Catholic, Anglican, United, and several other churches) helped Martínez find a temporary place to stay. They lent him money to pay back the workmates who had raised his travel funds, and got him a job in a clothing factory while his case was being considered. He found a place of his own—a filthy Rexdale apartment full of cockroaches, the best he could afford on his menial pay. Three or four dollars an hour would be riches in Guatemala, where the minimum wage is less than that *a day*. But he learned that the almighty dollar is far less mighty in its own countries than in his. The psychological problems continued. He was still frightened of Toyota jeeps. He still talked to himself. At last he made friends with a university professor who knew something about Central America; she invited him to live in her home.

"She is like my sister. She save me," Martínez says warmly in English. He glances around the room: tasteful prints on the walls, a fine record collection, shelves sagging with books. "Since I came to live here, my life start to change. She understand the effect of the persecution complex, paranoia—it takes a long time to go away. Then there is the blame that refugees feel, the guilt of the survivor. I think to myself, 'What have I done to deserve this when my friends and colleagues are being tortured and killed at home?' My dream, my hope is to go back to Guatemala, but if I go now for sure I'm going to be another 'disappeared' person or a dead man. So what can I do?" Martínez fixes me with a determined stare. "Little by little I start to tell the story. I go educating people who gradually become the voice for a people which has no voice—the people in Guatemala. That way I feel I'm doing something."

Guatemala is five times the size of El Salvador and nearly twice as populous. Half of all Central Americans are Guatemalans, yet their forested, volcano-studded land remains obscure, known (if at all) for ancient temples, Indian weaving, and extraordinary natural beauty. But its beauty hides tragedy the way music hides screams. By Canadian standards the country is densely inhabited—eight million people in an area one-tenth the size of Ontario—yet the land is rich. The problem is the way its riches are distributed.

Since the Spanish conquest, which began in 1524, Guatemala's wealth has been concentrated in fewer and fewer hands. The Maya Indians, heirs of a brilliant civilization, are still the ethnic majority—about 60 per cent of the population—but they have been relentlessly dispossessed. They live on fragmented plots of poor land, while great cash-crop plantations cover the best soil. No other country in Latin America has such an unequal landholding structure, which is saying a lot.

For the Maya, Guatemala's independence from Spain in 1821 was merely a white settler takeover, similar to what happened later in southern Africa. Like South Africa, Guatemala is a nation only on paper: a map line drawn around a collection of rival ethnic groups and fiercely antagonistic social classes. For most of its history the only political model has been the domination of the weak by the strong. In this sense it is a microcosm of the modern world: in Guatemala one sees clearly the full width of the gulf between North and South, the sweep of history from Europe's invasion of the Americas to modern civil war.

Guatemalans and other Latin Americans seek asylum in Canada because the United States does not welcome victims of regimes it supports. (Cubans, on the other hand, are admitted in droves.) In 1985 only 138 Central and South American refugees were let in officially by Washington; in the same year Canada took 4,459. Guatemalans began fleeing north with the latest surge of political unrest and guerrilla warfare at the end of the 1970s. Until three years ago, they had to make their way to Canada, or to an intermediate country, before applying for asylum. (By United

Nations definition, a refugee is a person *outside* his country of origin.) But in March 1984, the Canadian government moved to control the increasing flow: a visa requirement was imposed on all Guatemalan visitors, making it impossible for them simply to board an aircraft bound for Canada. At the same time the embassy in Guatemala City began to process refugees "internally", a procedure much the same as immigration, except that cases deemed urgent might be settled quickly by waiving normal criteria. Critics of the new system say that it exposes political refugees to unnecessary risks by funnelling them all through the capital, where a visit can alert their enemies.

The Canadian embassy occupies the fifth and sixth storeys of an office building on a traffic circle in fashionable Zone 9. You ride up in an elevator that stops at no other floors. At the top there's an armed policeman outside a heavy steel door; you have to ring a bell and shout your business into an intercom. Even I, Canadian passport in hand, was questioned closely before someone inside released the latch. There is admittedly a need for security in Guatemala: on January 31, 1980, thirty-nine people burned to death when police firebombed the Spanish embassy, which had been peacefully occupied by Indian leaders trying to publicize army atrocities in the countryside. But there's little doubt that the set-up at Canada's embassy deters many genuine refugees. One, now in Toronto, told me that she got past the police guard only because a sympathetic Mexican diplomat happened to arrive as she was being turned away.

In December 1985, just after the election of Guatemala's new civilian president, a woman named Beatriz Barrios was killed while trying to come to Canada. Her case focused attention on problems of procedure. It was said that Canadian bureaucrats moved too slowly. A former embassy official told me that Barrios had already been granted Canadian papers, and the fatal delay was in obtaining a Guatemalan passport and airline reservation.

Probably no one will ever know exactly what prompted her killers, but they evidently intended the theatrical brutality of her death to discourage other would-be *émigrés*. She was found naked and without hands, and a note on her corpse said "*Faltan Más*", "More to Come".

One Saturday afternoon, the auditorium of the public library in London, Ontario, is filled with the sound of Latin American folk music. This is no ordinary concert, but a study session intended to "break the silence" on Guatemala, the strange silence that enshrouds the country and its dead. Nightmare images occasionally reach North American media—mutilations, villages bombed, prisoners burned alive with gasoline, Indian babies used by troops as footballs—but the news dies almost as soon as it reaches the back pages. Silence returns. The murder of one priest in Poland attracts more attention than the murder of a dozen in Guatemala. South African president Botha's name becomes a byword for repression, but the military rulers of Guatemala have remained almost unknown while pursuing a level of state terror that makes South Africa's outrages seem mild. The Tutus and Mandelas of Guatemala have been dead for years.

The band members in London are a Chilean *charango* player, a Salvadorean guitarist, and two Guatemalan brothers, Victor and Alfredo Caxaj. Victor has a thick black beard and wavy hair to match; he plays guitar and a large drum. Alfredo is younger and cleanshaven, with the straight hair and elegant bone structure of the Maya forebears from whom their surname (pronounced "Cashah") comes. All wear white cotton trousers and green shirts of handwoven Guatemalan cloth. They blend Spanish harmonies with the warbling Andean flute played expertly by Alfredo; their songs denounce injustice and praise the popular struggle.

For the Caxajs that struggle is no abstraction. Their elder brother Carlos was assassinated outside his home in 1985, and their younger brother, Marco Antonio, kidnapped two and a half years before. They introduce me to their sister-in-law, Patricia de Caxaj, Marco Antonio's wife, who has just arrived in Canada. She herself began receiving death threats (often directed at her little boy) after becoming conspicuous in GAM, the Mutual Support Group formed by relatives of the "disappeared".

"I came as a refugee because I am afraid for my child. It doesn't matter to *them* that he's still only a baby—he is the son of his father, my husband, and they try to ... as they say ... finish off the seed." Patricia de Caxaj is a slender woman of twenty-six with high cheekbones and long black hair gathered in a clasp behind her head. Like her brothers-in-law she has hazel eyes. She seems frail, but there is a toughness in her gaze born of four years of anger, pain, and unrequited hope.

"The situation in Guatemala looks fine on the surface," she continues, while the band takes a break. "But underneath it is not so. The military still has control. President Vinicio Cerezo has said that he can do nothing for us, that we must forget the past. His wife has even told us to accept the fact that we are widows." For GAM members it is an article of faith that many of the disappeared are still alive, held somewhere in secret prisons. They use the present tense to refer to their vanished relatives; their slogan is "Alive they were taken, and alive we want them back."

A Canadian member of the local Guatemala Solidarity Committee gets up to announce that Patricia and her sister-in-law, Brisna (Carlos's widow), will give their testimony to the audience. About a hundred people have come. Half are Canadians, the rest from the same sad countries—Guatemala, El Salvador, Chile—as the band. The Latin Americans have their children with them, and the room is noisy, but as the women start to speak even the toddlers hush.

"On the twenty-ninth of December, 1982, on the day he returned to his job with the Ministry of Agriculture after our honeymoon, my husband, Marco Antonio Caxaj, was seized by heavily armed men who came in two cars. Witnesses noted the numbers of the plates, which were later traced to G2, the intelligence branch of the Guatemalan army. After he was taken we searched everywhere. We sent telegrams to the president ... we placed advertisements in the newspapers. His parents went to the Ministry of the Interior ... the colonel in charge told them they would disappear in the same way if they kept on making demands for his release."

By this point, Patricia de Caxaj has lost her composure, and in between sentences, while a Canadian translates, tears stream down her face. But she does not stop, and in defiance of her grief her voice grows louder as she finishes what she has to say. I wonder how many times she has forced herself to do this, to relive in public the events that shattered her life. Patricia is followed by Brisna, whose husband's fate was more recent and more final. She has been in Canada about a year and tells her story in halting English.

"On the twenty-ninth of July 1985, on his way home from work, Carlos was stopped by four heavily armed men, who shot him dead in the street without asking any questions...."

She too ends in tears. The monstrosity of Guatemala is in the room, an evil presence, summoned and shamed by the simple, difficult words. Guatemalans, I note, are very precise about dates—they quote the exact day of each murder and disappearance. Killings are sometimes timed precisely for maximum psychological effect: it was perhaps no accident that both Caxaj brothers were attacked on the same day of the month. I was reminded of a much earlier reign of terror in Guatemala—the first wave of oppression by Pedro de Alvarado, probably the most brutal of all the leading conquistadores. Then, too, the victims recorded each atrocity with precision, laconically setting down the dates in the Maya calendar:

On the day Four Lizard [March 9, 1524], the kings Ahpop and Ahpop Qamahay were burned to death by Alvarado. The heart of Alvarado had no pity for the people....

On the day Thirteen Rabbit [May 28, 1540], the Ahpo Zotzil king, Cahí Imox, was hanged by Alvarado, together with Quiyavit Caok....

After the Ahpo Zotzil king was hanged, they hanged Chuuy Tziquinú, lord of the city, because they were angry. On the day Four Serpent [March 1, 1541], they hanged him in Paxayá....

Seventeen days [later] Lord Chicbal and Nimabah Quehchun were hanged together, on the day Eight Wind.

The Spanish conquest is not forgotten in Guatemala. The Maya and their supporters trace the present oppression back more than 450 years. What distinguishes Guatemala from the rest of Central America, where Indians are largely extinct as a separate entity, is the way that racism has been recast as anti-communism. The intransigence of the powerful families, several of which are directly descended from conquistadores, is a cultural problem rooted in their inability to see Guatemala as anything other than a private fief. For them the Indians and lower classes are not fellow citizens, but a resource to be worked for maximum profit.

This *ancien régime* received fresh ideological transfusions from white supremacist German coffee planters who came in the nineteenth century, and social Darwinist foreign investors who came in the twentieth. Most recent investment is American, but Inco of Canada was heavily involved in the infamous Exmibal mining project, which displaced many Kekchí Maya from ancestral lands before it was shelved for economic reasons in 1981.

With the failure of land and political reforms, aborted by a CIA-directed coup in 1954, Guatemala has become a bastion of the ultra-right, a bunker of Latin Afrikanerdom. When the United States

Congress cut off military aid in 1977 for massive human rights violations, South Africa was conspicuous among Guatemala's few remaining friends.

The Guatemalan army has, by its own count, destroyed 440 villages in the counter-insurgency campaign. At the height of the fighting in 1982-83, Guatemala's bishops estimated that one million persons—one-quarter of the Maya population—had been displaced from their homes. But not many Indian refugees have made their way to Canada. The majority hid in the hills and forests or fled overland to Mexico, where about 100,000 still remain. Few had the desire, and fewer the opportunity, to apply for asylum further afield. Among the few Guatemalan Maya in Toronto, I met a young man I'll call Arcadio Balam. Involvement in a peasant organization forced him to leave. Balam was multilingual in three Maya languages and Spanish, and his English is now so accomplished that he's studying at university.

Most Guatemalans who reach Canada are from the Ladino ("Latin") sector of the population. This includes whites, those of mixed descent, and Indians assimilated by either choice or duress. Ladinos dominate the urban trades and professions, including politics, the army, and police. They speak Spanish, wear Western clothes, and identify with the "nation" of Guatemala—the same nation seen by most Indians as a cruel fiction, a thinly disguised colony built on their lands and backs. The very things that Guatemala projects to the outside world as its national image—the costumes and traditions of the Maya—are badges of second-class citizenship within the country. "What we need in Guatemala," Arcadio Balam told me, "is not just a political revolution, but a cultural one. We need education in our own languages, and respect for who we are."

The Mexican writer and diplomat Carlos Fuentes has spoken of the bankruptcy of ideologies and "re-emergence of cultures as protagonists of history". In Guatemala, ethnicity and ideology are endlessly confused. It is still unclear to what extent the recent insurgency was a genuine Maya uprising, or a Ladino civil war with Indians dragooned into fighting on both sides.

The band returned. They asked everyone to stand in respect for the disappeared, the dead, and other victims of oppression. They began to sing revolutionary songs, songs that echoed many civil wars: Mexico, Spain, Nicaragua. *Vamos muchachos, vamos a la montaña.* In religion the devil may have all the best tunes, but in Latin America it is the leftist revolutionaries. Guatemalan coffee planters have their own favourite: the *Horst Wessel Lied.*

Afterwards, I followed the Caxajs' old Plymouth from the graceful centre of London to a low-rent housing complex on the edge of the city. They live in dark brown cubes of brick surrounded by asphalt, parking stalls, and borders of trampled turf. We went up to the apartment shared by Victor, his wife, Vilma, their three young children, and Brisna, Carlos Caxaj's widow. They had done their best to brighten the scuffed walls with photographs and cheerful weavings from their homeland. The lime-green shag, as beaten as the turf outside, was half hidden by armchairs and a cascade of children's toys.

All the Guatemalan homes I saw in Canada had the same look: a home away from home, agreeable but impermanent. Weavings, posters, second-hand furniture—these things were not merely the result of poverty, but the choice of people who wish to remain mobile, unencumbered by belongings that cannot be jettisoned or put in suitcases. The Caxajs, like the others I spoke with, were grateful for what Canada had done for them, but they had no intention of staying here for ever and forgetting the past.

"We have to wait, but the thought of returning to our country is always with us," Victor said. "For us the story isn't over, for us being here is only a step. We know we must go back eventually—either because things have changed or, if they haven't, so that we can help them change." Most of the Caxaj family had been high-school teachers, prominent in the secondary teachers' association. Carlos was killed just three days after Victor had been elected association president.

"Obviously Victor would be the next," Brisna said, "so he left for Canada almost immediately. At first the rest of us thought we'd try to stay on. We wanted to go on protesting Carlos's death and the disappearance of Patricia's husband. We took part in some strikes and demonstrations. Soon we noticed that the secret police were following us. Every time I went out there were these men behind me. We realized we had better leave."

The apartment had filled with the aroma of toasted tortillas and fried beans. Vilma and Patricia called us to the formica dining table. Did I like Central American food? they asked. I dug in. The *tostadas* brought back memories of smoky eating houses built from rough-sawn planks beside the gravel roads of Guatemala, of clouds drifting across green volcanoes, the rank smell of the jungle. The memories didn't fit the austerity of the scene outside the window: leafless trees, rows of identical brick buildings, neon signs above a shopping centre, a cold sun too weak to warm the ground. The Caxajs had paid a high price for sanctuary.

I asked if they'd managed to find any outlet for their talents here.

"Vilma has a good job," Victor said. "She works in a daycare centre for Latin American children. But Alfredo and I are still taking English lessons. We can't teach, our qualifications aren't recognized. So we work with the Guatemala solidarity groups, we practise and play a lot of engagements with our band—to try and tell people about the situation in our country."

I had to ask *why?* Why do people go on protesting in Guatemala? Why do they continue to form unions and self-help groups when any form of organization brings kidnapping, torture, death, or exile?

"We were doing nothing wrong," Brisna said defiantly. "We broke no laws, we respected the constitution. We weren't communists. We are Christians."

"Besides," added Alfredo, "you can be persecuted in Guatemala for merely doing your job. Our younger brother, Marco Antonio—Patricia's husband—was an agronomist. He took his work seriously. He used to go out to the countryside and come back at the end of the day with mud on his boots. But his department, like all government departments at that time, was run by an army officer. This officer would come to the office at ten o'clock, sign a few papers, and go out at noon to drink cocktails for the rest of the day. My brother wasn't like that. He got up early, he did his work, he passed on the peasants' requests to the ministry. This was noticed by his boss: anyone who works that hard and stands up for the peasants must be a communist. That army officer sat in his office, pretending not to hear, as they dragged my brother away."

I asked them how Canadians reacted to their story. Of all the countries in this hemisphere, Canada and Guatemala must be about as different as it is possible to get. The one large, bland, new, safe, empty, and cold; the other tiny, crowded, ancient, tropical, culturally and geographically as convoluted as a brain. Could Canadians who had not visited Guatemala imagine the Dickensian poverty, the racism, the Hitlerish politics? Alfredo answered in English:

"Most Canadians are nice to us, but it is difficult for them to understand. It's like another world. They see the American TV, they often think Russia and Cuba are behind our country's problems. But the problem isn't communism. The problem is injustice, misery, the numbers of children who die every day from malnutrition and disease. The people who are fighting are the Indians and the poor. We've never seen a Russian or a Cuban in our country, but what we have seen is plenty of American military 'advisers.'"

The recent troubles in Guatemala can be traced directly to the 1954 coup, which ended a decade of democracy and ushered in thirty years of military rule. The coup was modelled on the CIA's Iranian intervention of 1953, and was itself a blueprint for the Bay of Pigs fiasco, the successful overthrow of Chile's President Salvador Allende in 1973, and the Contra war against the Nicaraguan government. Like Allende, Guatemalan president Jacobo Arbenz (1950-54) was freely elected but unacceptable to Washington because of left-wing tendencies. Unlike Allende, Arbenz himself was not a Marxist, though there were some communists in his administration. He might have been tolerated had he not tried to redistribute idle lands of the powerful United Fruit Company to landless peasants. United Fruit had close ties with the Dulles brothers, one of whom was the U.S. Secretary of State and the other the director of the CIA.

The big Guatemalan landowners were equally disturbed by the prospect of land reform, not only because it threatened their vast estates, but because land shortage was (and is) the principal force that drives Indians to migrate each year at harvest time to the coffee and cotton estates, where they suffer appalling conditions for minimal pay. Sometimes they are sprayed with pesticides as they work in the fields, resulting in deaths and miscarriages; seldom are they paid the minimum wage of U.S.$1.20 a day. Other thousands of Indians and poor Ladinos drift to Guatemala City's slums. The lucky ones swell the supply of cheap labour for foreign and domestic corporations. Most find no full-time employment, and survive by peddling, prostitution, or sifting through garbage dumps for the leavings of the rich. Study after study, before 1954 and since, has concluded that land reform is not only politically urgent but vital for the emergence of a modern economy. However, the elite, backed by hardliners in the army, has become increasingly hostile to social change.

It is difficult to grasp the extremism of the Guatemalan right.

Mario Sandoval, a veteran of the 1954 coup and a presidential candidate in the recent elections, once declared it might be necessary to kill half a million Guatemalans to "cleanse" the country of communism. In Guatemala that was no idle threat: since 1954 at least 100,000 Guatemalans have been murdered for political reasons; 38,000 more have disappeared; and about 200,000 have fled the country. Diplomatic and human rights sources agree that the bulk of this terror is the work of paramilitary organizations linked to the army, the police force, and far-right parties like Sandoval's ironically named National Liberation Movement.

In theory, Guatemala, like Argentina, has recently returned to democracy after a dark period of military rule. President Vinicio Cerezo, a Christian Democrat, won a convincing electoral victory in December 1985. In theory the government is now civilian, and constitutional guarantees have been restored. But Guatemala is not Argentina: the generals have not discredited themselves by losing a war. On the contrary, they pride themselves on defeating the guerrilla insurgents without American help. (Neither claim is quite true: resistance still exists, and President Reagan found ways to circumvent the congressional ban on military aid.) In 1985, Colonel Edgar D'Jalma Domínguez boasted to foreign journalists: "In Argentina there are witnesses, there are books, there are films, there is proof. Here in Guatemala there is none of that. Here there are no survivors."

Cerezo has very little political space; he exists only on the generals' sufferance—a fact he makes no attempt to deny. He himself admits that he holds no more than 30 per cent of the power, and that his main ambition is to survive his term of office. Many regard his election as nothing more than a cosmetic change tolerated by the military because of the desperate economic crisis; others believe that Cerezo has the chance to nurture a genuine democratic opening. Some have noted drily that the army may have returned to barracks, but the barracks is the whole of Guatemala.

At a small brick house with a sagging porch in the Parkdale district of Toronto, Alfredo Saavedra shows me a black and white photograph of himself between two colleagues: "The man on the left was captured by the army and killed in November 1979; the one on the right was the editor of a newspaper I worked for. A death squad killed him in March 1982."

Saavedra was a prominent journalist and poet. He fled after his name appeared on a death list.

"Guatemala is a great exporter of culture," he said ironically, reminding me that Latin America's first winner (in 1967) of the Nobel Prize for Literature, Miguel Angel Asturias, was a Guatemalan. Saavedra prefers to describe himself as an exile, rather than a refugee, because he came to Canada indirectly after working for a spell in Honduras as a press-service correspondent. He speaks softly in elegant, formal Spanish, choosing his words deliberately. His eyes explore a middle distance filled with images and ideas.

Journalism was Saavedra's career, but his real love is literature. He shows me reviews of the books he published in Guatemala. One was a collection of his poetry, called *Declaración Jurada* (*Sworn Statement*), in which this verse appears:

They put up their hands
From obedience or from fear.
They sought and did not find,
They asked for bread and were given a stone…
Others asked for peace
And they received it in the grave.

Politics in Guatemala have a cyclical history. Whenever the powers that be feel secure, there is a tendency to relax the repression and allow a few democratic trappings to appear, mainly for international consumption. During these periods dissenting voices such as Saavedra's are allowed to emerge. Then, when opposition becomes too organized and strident, a fresh wave of killings and disappearances destroys the leadership. Guatemala allows the grass roots to sprout and then mows the lawn.

As Saavedra talks it becomes clear that one of his greatest burdens is isolation—the isolation that envelops a man of words deprived of expression. "I have felt very deeply that we artists and intellectuals from Latin America are not listened to here in Canada. The presence of our culture could enrich the Canadian culture around us, but instead we are wanted only for our manpower as factory workers and janitors—to do the jobs no Canadians want." He sweeps his hand around the small living room, filled with sagging furniture and a large cabinet television from the 1960s. Photos of his children smile down from the walls. "You know, in my country I used to live much better than this. No one can say I came to Canada to raise my standard of living."

Guatemala does not honour its prophets. Countless intellectuals have joined the country's haemorrhage; two of the last three rectors of the university have been killed. Perhaps the hardest irony for those like Saavedra is that in Guatemala their prominence made them victims, and in exile they are victims of obscurity.

There are perhaps four or five thousand Guatemalan exiles in Canada. But they are no more a community than their country is a nation. I found fragments, small networks of individuals trusting only the ties of blood and friendship. They are wary of each other, believing, rightly or wrongly, that some of their compatriots may be *orejas*—"ears"—who listen and report.

Almost all the refugees I spoke to are adamant that they will not return until their country is truly free. Almost all are determined that they will not assimilate into Canadian society and forget. Not until the Guatemalan army is tried for its crimes, and the Vietnam-style strategic hamlets in which many Indians are confined have been abolished, will they be convinced that real progress has come to Guatemala. The refugees are not inclined to give the benefit of the doubt; they have seen too many reforms end in blood. This is a dilemma: President Cerezo's democratic opening is, in their own view, doomed to fail, and guerrilla defeat of the ruthless and well-equipped Guatemalan army now appears more remote than ever. Yet I met none who admitted to despair. The belief in a new Guatemala is religious, intense, and basic to survival. The adults, and those without family here, will likely maintain this determination all their lives, or until their hopes are met. But for the children, Guatemala fades with every year that goes by.

Ricardo and Lidia Xajil (pronounced "Shaheel") live in a basement apartment on a busy Toronto thoroughfare. Over the couch there's a picture of the ancient pyramids at Tikal, which the Xajils, like most poorer Guatemalans, have never visited. The magnificent ruined city is a powerful symbol: for the Maya, a memorial of greatness; for the white elite, a spurious identification with the conquered race—like the Canadian pride in totem poles. Above the dining table is another image, a parody of a tourist poster. It reads: GUATEMALA: THE LAND OF ETERNAL REPRESSION.

"We try always to keep the idea of returning to Guatemala alive in the minds of our children," Ricardo Xajil tells me. "But we've been here five years now. Even for the eldest that is more than half his life. The kids adapt far more quickly than we do. That is our greatest worry." He sighs, and glances at the two good-looking boys playing on the floor. "*¡Están olvidando la lengua!* They are forgetting the language. It's more and more difficult to make them speak in Spanish."

For this family it would be the second loss of language in three generations. Their grandparents spoke Quiché and Cakchiquel—closely related Maya languages with nearly two million speakers all told. Assimilation into Ladino Guatemala is not far in the Xajils' past; now they face a second transformation into gringos.

"I miss very much our customs, the family ties," Lidia says. "Here we live in this apartment building, but we have no contact with any of the neighbours. We feel boxed in, we feel isolated."

Another parent I met was more outspoken: "We feel the alienation of the gringo culture. I don't want my kids to be formed in a country so close to Disneyland and Rambo."

Rambo bothers many exiled Guatemalans. That very morning I had seen a catalogue of Christmas toys. It featured something called the Rambo Collection: "the Force of Freedom, trained experts who risk their lives for freedom's cause." Guatemala has experienced the freedom offered by Rambo—freedom to choose only the American way.

The Xajils, like the Caxajs, try to keep their culture and their rage alive by playing in a band. The one substantial piece of furniture in their apartment is a fine marimba, the traditional wooden xylophone of Guatemala. Beneath it is a *tun*, a wooden drum of pre-Columbian design.

"Originally we formed the band because we wanted to commemorate those who died in the burning of the Spanish embassy," Ricardo says. "We try to carry a message, a cultural message and a political message, and to keep in touch with things from our homeland."

Guatemalans have great faith in the power of culture, whether as literature, music, or a system of belief. Within Guatemala the Maya have learned to use culture as a form of resistance, a stronghold from which to face a terrible invasion. That same stronghold now helps exiled Guatemalans of all ethnic backgrounds resist the forces of Disneyland. The question is: how long can it work for them in a foreign country?

The Xajils have saved enough from their low-paying jobs (his in a sheet-metal factory, hers at a sewing machine) to buy a car.

Once a year they drive down through Mexico to the town of Tapachula on the Guatemalan border. Other families make the same pilgrimage, furtively, posing as tourists. There they meet parents and cousins, who cross over for a brief reunion. The bolder exiles walk half-way across the international bridge for a longing glimpse of the homeland that might kill them if they made a premature return. Then they get into their cars, loaded with gifts and memories, turn round, and begin the journey back to Canada. They are prepared for a long wait.

SIX

An Antique Land

It took me fifteen years to contemplate that triumph of hope over experience: a second marriage. A travelling life not only makes attachments difficult, it easily becomes an excuse for avoiding them. My new wife, Janice Boddy, was a veteran traveller herself. She had earned her doctorate in anthropology after long periods of fieldwork in a remote part of Sudan. We'd known each other years before in Calgary—she'd entered the university there about the time that I dropped out—but had lost touch until we both moved, independently, to Toronto. We got married after one of my trips to Central America.

At about this time the Toronto *Globe and Mail* launched *Destinations*, a travel magazine. Jack McIver, the founding editor, soon made *Destinations* known for its writing. He sought out novelists, poets, and other literary travellers. A dapper man who always wore a blazer or a suit, he would say to his authors, "I never travel. Your job is to save me the trouble. Go and write about anything you want—so long as it takes me there."

Janice and I had wanted to return to Egypt ever since making a boat trip down the Nile after one of her stays in Sudan. I persuaded Jack to send us back there for his magazine, pointing out that my wife, who spoke fluent Arabic, would be an ideal dragoman.

GRAND ANTIQUITIES are like great films: the clutter and banality of life are stripped away and we are left with the compelling image, the larger-than-life character, the sunset more beautiful than any belonging to the quotidian world. This is the Egypt we have always known—from childhood stories, coffee-table books, nineteenth-century lithographs on study walls. The temples and tombs are a vast outdoor museum, more cunningly contrived and displayed than all the fragments of Egyptian glory crammed into the halls of Cairo, London, or New York. Those old pharaohs knew their business: it was immortality they wanted and immortality they got. *Look on my works, ye Mighty, and despair!* Well, despair is perhaps for those who wish to emulate. Caesar, Napoleon, Hitler, Mao—they might come and feel despair that it had all been done before. Some took away an obelisk or two. But mostly they took images and ideas: the colossal face of the god-king, serene, implacable, ineluctable. This was Egypt's legacy: the making of man into god, the setting of solar distance between ruler and ruled, the focusing of national adoration on a superman.

But we, an ordinary man and woman from a demotic time and place, what do we feel? There is wonder, yes, but the wonder is curdled with fear. Not for nothing do modern Egyptians call the Sphinx *Abu Huul*, Father of Terror. And the terror is all the worse for the smile playing about the beast's eroded lips: the smile of a Mona Lisa or the smile of a torturer, who can say? If you go to the *son et lumière* at the Pyramids (the world's first and possibly the worst) you will hear a famous voice—Charlton Heston's, I think—speaking the words of the Sphinx. I have watched five thousand years! says the Sphinx, who ends every sentence with an exclamation mark. I have seen Egyptian, Ethiopian, Greek, and

Roman emperors come and go! I was old when Moses was pulled from his basket in the reeds by Pharaoh's daughter, when Herodotus came to see me, when Rome fell and Islam arose!

But we can never look at the Sphinx without thinking of that ditty:

The sexual urge of the camel
Is greater than anyone thinks,
After weeks and weeks in the desert
It makes an assault on the Sphinx.
But the Sphinx's eternal orifice
Is blocked with the sands of the Nile,
Which accounts for the hump on the camel
And the Sphinx's inscrutable smile.

Then in the pink and orange spotlights we see a fly on the Sphinx's nose. But it is not a fly, it's a pigeon, and the enormity of the creature, its age and size, crash down again on our irreverent minds. If we date our civilization from the Renaissance, Egypt has existed ten times as long; if we count our years from the birth of Christ, the Sphinx was already older then than Christianity is now. And it takes only a little delving into Egypt's religion to find evidence of plagiarism by the younger faith. Consider Osiris, a god who grew up as a man, who was murdered by his enemies, briefly resurrected upon earth, and then ascended into heaven where he sits in judgement of the dead.

The Pyramids have not been diminished by the Cairo suburbs massing at their gate—if anything, the sunsets have been improved by the pollution—but we do not return. Once is enough for that geometry lesson in stone. The Pyramids hold no surprise beyond the initial shock of their immensity. How many times do we need to be reminded of a pharaoh's mania and the sweat and blood of thousands who slaved in the sun to commemorate it? You look at the whole Giza complex, at its grandiose assertion of culture over nature, and you have to agree with what Alexander Woollcott said about the formal grounds of a friend's country house: "just what God would have done if he'd had the money."

We go instead to Upper Egypt, and check into Aswan's Old Cataract Hotel, familiar from the film of Agatha Christie's *Death on the Nile* (the outside, anyway; interior shots were filmed elsewhere). Its late Victorian façade, russet stucco with white trim, looks out over granite boulders worn smooth by Nile floods. Directly opposite lies Elephantine Island, named for the appearance of the rocks, and through the narrow channel glide the white gullwings of felucca sails. We are given a vast room on the third floor, its french doors opening to a balcony with a view of many ages. On the crest of the island stands a small Old Kingdom pyramid, built around 2600 B.C.; directly opposite is a Roman quay incorporating much older stones with scrambled hieroglyphs; in the distance, a house built by Lord Kitchener when he invaded Sudan in the late 1890s; and above, on the skyline, the domed mausoleum of the Aga Khan who died in 1957.

It is evening now and the clichés of Egyptian travel are coming to life: a beet sun falling into the haze above desert hills, felucca sails limp in the still air, songs of the boatmen and the plash of their oars in tea-dark water, a muezzin calling from a minaret, a whisky bottle and two glasses on our wicker table.

The dining is a disappointment. Like most Egyptian hotels, the Old Cataract is still trying to master the sort of food the British liked forty years ago—greasy stews full of gristle, cadaverous chips (colder than the beer), cakes and tarts glowing with artificial colour, and toast like damp acoustic ceiling tile. One look at this and we take our chances under the stars on the corniche—a cheeky bottle of Château Ptolemy rosé and a shish kebab with rice marred only by some telltale grains clinging to the corner of our waiter's mouth.

Janice suggests we walk off the meal in the souk, a labyrinth of lanes and tiny shops lit by neon tubes. Gold neon bathes a jewellery store the size of a broom cupboard; velvet-red a draper's shop; crocus-yellow a mountain of spice baskets spilling into the street. Nubian housewives, portly as seals and wrapped in black from head to ankle, are feeling fabrics, sniffing meat. There are dim, smoky cafés where young men drink tea in glasses and old men puff on narghiles. Smells of cinnamon, tobacco, coriander leaves, and drains; sounds of a dozen radios playing the same warbling quarter-tones; a donkey's bray; the fart of a motorbike.

"Welcome my country!"

"Thank you."

"What country, pliss?"

"Canada."

"Canada Dry! My name Yusuf."

Yusuf wears a flowing jellaba made of striped pyjama cloth, and a white turban that looks like a bandage for a head wound. He has brilliant, gold-capped teeth and a Zapata moustache.

"Yes! Welcome my shop!"

He wants to make me a cotton shirt with my name spelled in hieroglyphs on the pocket, or a dress, ditto, for Janice. He has leather bags, brass trays, onyx eggs, and pyramids. Or, if we prefer something more ethnic, a pile of dusty camel saddles and a drawer full of horns, hoofs, and skins from dwindling species.

"*Mumkin nashuf?*" asks Janice. "May we just look?" This has the usual impact: shock, followed by laughter at her rustic accent. (I try to imagine the effect of a Sudanese speaking broad Lancashire in London.) She wants a *rik*, a Nubian tambourine. Yusuf rummages in the back and brings her a small instrument inlaid with bone, or possibly white plastic.

"Twenty-five bounds!" he shouts (Arabic speakers have trouble with the letter p). Janice offers *ashara*—ten. The rest is predictable. He paid twenty for it himself! But just for madame...

because she speaks Arabic … eighteen—a gift! The price falls further: seventeen … sixteen … my last price! Janice offers fifteen. A crestfallen Yusuf nods and starts counting off change from a roll of banknotes like scraps of brown Kleenex held together with tape. The glittering teeth disappear, the moustache droops in sorrow. "So cheap. Perhaps … a pen?" Janice hands him a ballpoint. Yusuf's teeth reappear—red, green, and blue in the neon lights.

It's a short hop by plane to Abu Simbel, moved in the 1960s when the water rose behind the Aswan dam. (Originally carved in the living sandstone of the Nile gorge, the temples had to be sawn into thirty-ton blocks and reassembled.) For 200 miles the drowned river lies beneath us—an inert expanse of quicksilver between low, barren hills—stretching on to the Sudanese border and beyond. So very different, Janice remarks, from the silty, palm-lined Nile that glides past the village where she lived north of Khartoum.

The façade with its four seated colossi of Rameses, each sixty feet high, is almost as familiar as the image of the Pyramids. Here again is that chilling smile, and lest we are not quite sure what Rameses is smiling about, bound captives from Asia and Africa parade miserably along the base of his pedestal. Perhaps he is also smiling at the presence of his family. Their figures are tiny compared to his, though they would be major sculptures anywhere else. Here are his mother, several wives, and some favourite children, including the princess Bent-Anat, who became a wife as well as a daughter. Rameses had more than 200 children all told, which makes one wonder why his name is used by a well-known brand of condom.

Between Aswan and Luxor, which we do by car, are several Ptolemaic temples. Edfu, the largest and best preserved, is hemmed in by a modern town built on the sand that buried it and saved it from destruction. Mudbrick houses, festoons of laundry, and TV aerials rather spoil the temple's dignity, and we are badgered by guards stealthily offering to take us up on the roof, or open a "secret" passage—which they themselves have just blocked—for a tip.

But Kom Ombo sits among irrigated fields with the Nile washing its feet. Some of the columns and lintels are still bright with green, red, blue, and yellow paint, reminding you that all these sandstone walls were once covered with a visual luxuriance that nature denies this desert land. The ancient Egyptians loved colour, and the modern ones—especially the Nubians resettled near here after Lake Nasser drowned their villages—paint the outsides of their houses with bright mementoes of pilgrimages to Mecca: a yellow bus; a silver Boeing; the black-draped Kaaba with its mysterious stone at the centre of the Muslim world.

Exquisite bas reliefs on the temple walls reveal the curves of breasts and thighs, the rippling muscles of legs and torsos. Unlike Islam, ancient Egypt was not afraid to show the human body, although most of these lissom gods have the heads of animals. Especially prominent are the lords of Kom Ombo: Harwer, a falcon deity, and Sobek, the crocodile. Sacred crocodiles were kept in a huge well entered by a tunnel and spiral stair, and in a small side chapel we see their mummies stacked like rotten logs. Kom Ombo's gods still have some worshippers—a score of half-dressed Californians are sitting, lotus posture, on the precinct walls.

Across the Nile from Luxor—the city the Greeks called Thebes—are the arid valleys of the Kings and Queens, where royalty were buried in painted tombs cut deep into the cliffs. (The building of pyramids declined after about 2500 B.C.) There's no bridge to the west bank, but several ferryboats scuttle back and forth like smoky water beetles. There we make a deal with a cabby called Nasr for all day. Nasr's receding hairline gives him an intellectual air, and Janice engages him in conversation. It isn't long before he produces a wad of dog-eared letters, evidence of a steamy affair with an American tourist. Such Egyptians tend to assume that all foreign women are available; to judge from Nasr's letters, sometimes they are right. We invent five children to dispel any notion that Janice might be in search of a real (i.e. Egyptian) man.

"What about antiques?" Nasr asks next. "You want to buy?"

"No, thank you, they're forbidden."

"Why is that?"

"Because the government says antiquities belong in museums."

"Ah!" says Nasr. "That's because they're old. But *new* antiques are all right. You want to visit my friend's antique shop?"

Once the ground rules are established—no cuckoldry, no artifacts—Nasr fulfils his bargain, taking us to the tombs, several temples, and the Colossi of Memnon—two figures of Amenhotep III sitting regally beside the road, their faces eaten by the wind of thirty-three centuries.

Every British schoolchild knows Shelley's "Ozymandias", so it's quite a thrill to see the "colossal wreck" thought to have inspired him. This statue of Rameses is in the Ramesseum, a temple built for the pharaoh's cult after death. Carved originally from a single block of grey granite, it lies in great chunks as if blown apart by dynamite. Only the feet seem to be in the original position, side by side on the sand like a pair of slippers, each about ten feet long. The torso has lost its forearms and someone tried to saw through the head centuries ago. But the hard stone retains its polish, giving these dismembered bits of Rameses the musclebound, oiled look of a Greek athlete or a hero of socialism.

Half sunk, a shattered visage lies, whose frown,
And wrinkled lip, and sneer of cold command,

Tell that its sculptor well those passions read
Which yet survive, stamped on these lifeless things...

Wherever you see Rameses—so much larger and more muscular than anyone else; so much more virile, victorious, pious, and wise—you sense the insecurity that lay behind all these pompous statements and their modern imitations. Egypt was a one-track land, hemmed in by the sands on either side and even more by disdain for foreigners and their ideas. (She took 2,000 years to adopt the wheel from Mesopotamia.) It is as if dependence on the straight and narrow Nile circumscribed her intellect and imagination, producing a rigid, dogmatic personality. After each period of chaos or invasion, old patterns re-established themselves. Over and over again, the same message was hammered home: one people, one empire, one pharaoh. It is a message still to be heard and feared, whether from the lips of stone colossi or of modern demagogues: *ein Volk, ein Reich, ein Führer.*

The tombs are less forbidding than the temples. Their walls glow with charming murals of godly and daily life: a blind harpist, a row of baboons singing to the sunrise, and in the burial chamber above the sarcophagus, the long slim body of Nut, the sky goddess, who swallows the sun at night and gives birth to it each morning. Tutankhamun's famous grave is the size of a bachelor flat.

I don't like sound-and-light shows but Janice does, defending her taste on lofty ethnological grounds—something to do with seeing the uses to which the present puts the past. We take a calèche to Karnak for the evening performance, which I have to admit is better than I expected. The Karnak temple is so vast and ponderous, so cluttered with accretions and debris of different periods, that the spotlights impose an order invisible by day. At most ancient sites, *son et lumière* is a vulgar intrusion, but Karnak's grandiosity seems suited to the medium. If the priests of

Amun had had electricity, I'm sure they would have done the same.

Luxor Temple is more comprehensible than the vaster ruins at Karnak. It was also dedicated to Amun—but to a different aspect associated with fertility and often shown with penis ready for action. Long after Karnak was abandoned, Luxor remained a site of worship for many different ages and religions. The Romans built a basilica here, so did the Copts, and early Muslims perched a rustic mosque on the silt of centuries, against a pylon from the reign of Rameses.

As we leave the temple we are approached by an Egyptian:

"Monsieur! Mister! Monsieur!"

It turns out he has something interesting to offer—in his hand are keys to the tall minaret of a modern mosque that overlooks the entire temple complex and much of Luxor town.

"Up there, very good bicture! Luxor Tembel and Nile River, very nice!"

Janice looks at me and we both look at the concrete minaret. It's about 150 feet high with windows on all four sides near the top. For once, it seems, baksheesh would be well spent.

"How much?" I ask. He waves the suggestion of money away like a fly. We follow him into the mosque by a side entrance, then through another small door and up an iron spiral staircase that seems to go on for ever. The view at the top is indeed spectacular: everything we've been promised, plus, in the haze across the river, a suggestion of Hatshepsut's columned temple below lion-coloured cliffs. We shoot a few pictures and follow our entrepreneurial muezzin back down the trembling stairs. I get out two pounds—a generous tip by local standards. But at the bottom the door is locked and our friend has been joined by another.

"You must make a contribution to Allah," says the second man, who seems by his solemn manner and the Quran in his hand to be some sort of holy man. He taps a large wooden collection box. "Allah!" he repeats, as if God Himself were cooped up inside like a genie. I offer the two pounds. Outrage passes over the holy man's bearded face. "You can't give Allah two pounds!" He produces a ten-pound note from the folds of his jellaba and shakes it under my nose. "Allah!" He taps the box again.

After much bargaining, Allah settles for a fiver. The holy man then places a hand on my head, opens his Quran, and recites a verse, either in blessing or to neutralize my infidel presence. Another five pounds are extracted from Janice, another verse read, and the minaret door is unlocked. We are invited to wash our hands at the mosque fountain. We make a move for the street door, but it too is locked. "Now!" says the first man, dangling the keys, "now baksheesh for us."

It occurs to me, as we escape from the mosque, that the masses of ancient Egypt did not toil in vain. For as long as there is such a thing as tourism, they have bequeathed a living to their heirs.

SEVEN

Anatolian Badlands

Long after *Equinox* published my piece on Lamanai, the article bore an unexpected plum. The Turkish government and UNESCO decided to hold an international press seminar as part of a campaign to rescue Turkey's ancient monuments. Those invited were offered free travel to Istanbul, luxurious accommodation in the venerable Pera Palace Hotel, countless state banquets, and a tour of the rock-hewn cities and churches of Cappadocia. The Turks sought writers who had covered similar topics before, so when they approached *Equinox* my name came up. The *quid-pro quo* was publicity for the restoration programme, which needed to raise millions of dollars to save the monuments.

The only problem was that *Equinox* didn't want to do anything on Turkey. I could not in good conscience go on the trip without lining up a home for at least one article. My honour was saved when Jack McIver agreed to take a piece on Cappadocia for *Destinations.*

I'D NEVER RIDDEN in a bus with a police escort before. It seemed somehow appropriate for visiting a part of Asia Minor where outposts of Byzantine Europe had been driven underground; where churches, monasteries—even whole cities—had been hollowed from the rock to escape imperial pogroms and waves of conquest. It is easy to forget that half of the Roman Empire outlived Rome by a thousand years at Europe's eastern end. Not until 1453 did Constantinople fall like a great, dead oak to the Ottoman Turks. For centuries before and since that date, what is now Turkey has been the frontier separating East and West, the border land where countless battles between Islam and Christendom have been fought.

Turkey's many strata of history and culture are shuffled like the pages of an overflowing archive which is often ransacked and consulted but never set in order—so many peoples and times and faiths that it's all a bit too much. Only yesterday, in the Topkapı Palace, I'd seen an arm of John the Baptist and a hair from the Prophet's beard. The day before, I had stood in the dark, frigid air beneath the great dome of Haghia Sophia, the Holy Wisdom—once a church, then a mosque, now a museum—in a city known through different ages as Istanbul, Constantinople, Byzantium, and New Rome. And that great church, opened by Justinian in 537, was young beside monuments built before the Roman Empire split in two; and the city was itself a newcomer compared to Ephesus and Troy.

The escort for the bus was merely to get us through the rush-hour traffic of Ankara, a grim modern city on a Roman site, which replaced Constantinople as Turkey's capital when Kemal Atatürk imposed a new order in the 1920s. Anyone who has lived in Denver or Calgary might feel at home in Ankara. A cluster of high-rise buildings stands at the edge of a bald plain surrounded by brown hills. Frozen winds tore across the Anatolian steppes. It was almost May and the ground was speckled with snow. Efforts had been made to plant trees, but the pines were still too young and too regular to take the hard edge off the landscape. Yet the sun was fierce whenever it broke through roiling clouds and the smoke from thousands of coal fires. The snow did not melt; it simply transpired into the thin air.

We were a motley group: Philippe, a French intellectual with hair like Einstein's and jackets like Jimmy the Greek's; Tony, an Australian who looked and sounded like Paul Hogan; a Parisian doyenne known only as Madame Le Monde (because she was from *Le Monde*); an African; an Englishman; an American; a fragile beauty from Thailand; a compulsive shopper from Algeria; compulsive photographers from Japan. All of us were sustained on a regime of grand antiquities, formal speeches, Lucullan feasts, rivers of alcohol, and not much sleep. I envied those travellers who could eat when they were hungry, speak when they felt like it, and stay in bed when they were tired. "The trouble with the Turks, you know," the Englishman said wearily, "is that they *always* overdo things."

The bus trip eastward from Ankara to Cappadocia reminded me of going Greyhound across the prairies. You could doze off for hours, wake up, and everything outside the window was still the same: vast wheatfields tilled by invisible machines; skeletal poplars; patches of snow on the uplands; occasionally a glassy lake indistinguishable from a mirage. Then, very gradually, the land began to change. The fields got smaller; villages appeared; you saw goats and sheep, women in trousers and headscarves, stone houses with sod roofs. The country was more rolling, more broken by ravines. A barnacle-shaped volcano reared up on the eastern horizon, flying a pennant of cloud from its tip. Another appeared, further away and to the south.

Just beyond the provincial capital of Nevşehir the plain was scooped, cracked, gouged, and dotted with colossal hoodoos. Alberta's dinosaur country is a scale model compared to this. The eastern volcano's base was visible now, a white crinoline floating above rock pinnacles and deep, desolate canyons. You could see what had happened: millions of years ago the volcanoes—Mount Erciyes (ancient Argaeus) and Hasan Dagı—had erupted and covered this corner of Anatolia with deep deposits of ash capped by lava and basalt. The ash had compacted into tuff, a light, meringue-like stone. Then the weather broke through the hard mantle and began to carve what lay beneath, creating some of the most extravagant badlands on earth. Wherever chunks of lava remained they protected the lighter stone, forming wizards' hats, fezzes, mitres, yarmulkas, busbies, and Kaiser helmets on top of towers, cones, and columns. The pinnacles stand singly, in pairs, small groups, and long processions of robed figures. Some have a boulder perched on top like a ball on a seal's nose; lesser individuals who lost their headgear have been whittled into snouts, tipis, humps, and saddles. Some are distinctly phallic; others resemble swollen breasts tugged against gravity towards the sky. Whatever thoughts they may stir in the minds of travellers, these formations are known locally as "fairy chimneys".

It was evening. The hoodoos were turning a deep ochre, the gullies filled with purple light and pools of charcoal shadow. At first the landscape had seemed utterly alien and hostile to human life. But as the bus descended, entering it, one noticed that the hills and outcrops were riddled with holes like Emmental, that the holes had been houses, fortifications, and storage chambers. Around and below these carious massifs were modern towns, the living parts, as it were, of an ancient reef. Slim minarets and television aerials bristled against a crimson sky.

We were put up for several nights at Ürgüp. Half the town is in a valley, the other half roosts in surrounding cliffs. The back rooms of many houses are caves, and the free-standing walls of their façades are built from blocks of the same yielding stone, sometimes carved with cornices and crisp arabesques. On our beds we found gifts from the governor and the mayor: a bottle of local wine (not unlike Château Tanunda, according to Tony); some handicrafts; and a picture book of Cappadocia. The words of the book had an effect similar to the wine: "Cappadocia is a geological poem written by time, by million-yeared wind and water.... This high scherzo of nature transported calls the traveller to delirious voyaging. But watch your head."

As usual we were given a formal dinner. The governor of Nevşehir made a welcoming speech resounding with the natural and artistic treasures of Cappadocia. These things, he pointed out, were on the United Nations World Heritage List—a list of about 300 outstanding works of man and nature, including the Parthenon, Machu Picchu, and Head-Smashed-In Buffalo Jump. The world had rallied to the cause of Egypt's Aswan temples, threatened by the High Dam twenty years ago; now the frescoed churches of Cappadocia were equally at risk from the slow death of erosion, the quick death of thoughtless visitors and outright vandalism. He raised his glass to the campaign: would the world come to the aid of Turkey with the $76 million needed to rescue these churches and the historic monuments of Istanbul? The Australian was called upon to reply. Tony had evidently enjoyed his bottle of the local plonk, to say nothing of the *raki* (a sort of ouzo) and red wine supplied with the dinner's innumerable courses.

"Yeah," he began, cheerily saluting the governor with his glass. "Yeah. I think I can honestly say we've had a dinner that would slay a dingo. And of course we're looking forward to visiting the painted churches and all that. But I reckon any sights we see'll be pushed to top the belly dancer they laid on for us last night. Now *there* was a Turkish treasure."

I got up early next morning to find the ground covered by a

skiff of snow and the roofs of the town all white, reflecting a silver glare from the sunlight on the clouds round Mount Argaeus. A gaunt scene, more Nepalese than Turkish; we might have been far above the treeline in a remote corner of the Himalayas. A curtain of night had come down on the cheese and butter colours of yesterday, and today it had lifted on platinum and grey.

We crawled through an entire monastery carved into the cliffs at Göreme, something like a sandcastle turned inside out. The refectory was a rectangular cave with a table and benches hewn from the living rock. I'm sure all the monks had piles and nasty fungus infections that wouldn't go away. But they made wine here in stone vats and kept their cheeses and candles and whatever else monks keep in little stone shelves and cubbyholes. Now only the soot from centuries of candlelit dining remains—a low black ceiling that bruises and blackens your head. The kitchen still smells like a wet campfire, and when you go back outside the light is so dazzling you feel as if the earth had moved closer to the sun. How old? No one can really say. The churches have been dated by painting and architectural styles, but the unadorned troglodytic monasteries could have been built any time, perhaps even when Saint Basil the Great, who died in 379, was bishop of nearby Caesarea.

Monasticism flourished in Cappadocia for a thousand years; some of the churches were still in use when Greece and Turkey exchanged minority populations in 1923. The Turks are a little evasive about that. Islam forbids representation of the human form, and these churches filled with saints and Virgins and the awful face of Christ Pantocrator were seen as blasphemies by local zealots. At various times—perhaps the fifteenth century, perhaps (let it be said) the twentieth—stones were thrown at the Christian idols. But not all the blame can be laid on Muslims. During the Iconoclastic period from 726 to 843, the Byzantine emperors themselves forbade religious images. The superb mosaics of

Haghia Sophia were covered with plaster, and the early frescoes they had inspired in Cappadocia were painted over with spare geometric motifs.

Zeus, who was here long before Jesus or Mohammed, still does damage too. A few years ago lightning struck the church of El Nazar, a cruciform basilica cut within a solitary cone of tuff. The old church exploded. Chunks flew off its sides, exposing the delicately painted interior like a core of amethyst. Now the vaults hang in mid-air, roofs without walls, and the crypt where the bones were kept is open to prying eyes. From down there in the sacred basement you look up through a hole in the floor to the central dome, straight into the shattered face of God.

But there was one shrine that awaited us like an undiscovered royal tomb: Karanlık Kilise, the Dark Church. You enter through a great monastic hall that has fallen away, leaving only a few inner rooms and a false arcade marching across a precipice. A winding staircase tunnelled through the rock leads up into … what? No lights have been installed and you must follow on faith, one worn step after another, until you emerge in an echoing space like a sea-cave reached after an underwater swim. Torches play across domes and vaults and pillars, every inch covered in butterfly colours and designs. But not really—the butterflies are angels with golden haloes and blood-red wings; they fly against a blue-black sky, circling a ring of Greek script that orbits the dome, and in the middle of the Word is Christ, one hand holding a golden Bible, the other making a religious gesture used in our age for advertising pizza. There's a cinematic quality to these images that invites comparisons like that: the colours, preserved by darkness, are in technicolour; the scenes banner the faith. All these rolled eyes and trampled demons and sage apostles tugging at their beards are here to tell us something; not to mystify but to explain. Anthropomorphic cattle stare with beady, knowing eyes at the Child swaddled in a wicker basket. The Last Supper table has been set with knives and forks. It's the Bible by an eleventh-century Disney.

Here the Turks have begun restoration on their own, and the results show what could be done if the millions requested from UNESCO's campaign ever materialize. As it is, the budget allows the restorers to work only a few weeks each season, while rain and frost and carelessness operate all the time, slowly obliterating the achievements of a thousand years. It's one of history's ironies that this land, once the realm of Croesus, the Lydian king who is said to have invented money and certainly had a lot of it, now must stimulate the generosity of wealthy foreigners to save its past.

The sun climbs and sweeps the shadows under the rocks. I notice wildflowers and fruit trees in bloom. Against all appearances the land is fertile, and, against injunctions of the Prophet, Cappadocians find it excellent for grapes. Small terrace walls make stairs of the ravines, each step a level patch of soil for a dozen vines or apple trees. On the clifftops, silhouettes: old women and little girls, wrapped like mummies, driving flocks of sheep across what remains of the lava plateau.

We drank Turkish coffee at Üçhisar in a warm and lively tavern hollowed from the bedrock. Maybe the monks didn't live so badly after all.

One doesn't need much imagination to guess that life in the subterranean city of Kaymaklı cannot have been so pleasant. I wouldn't choose to live on the eighth storey, especially when it's the eighth below ground and the people on the other seven floors have their cows and goats with them. Then there are the communal latrines—huge shafts that end up somewhere near the eighth floor—to say nothing of food scraps, washwater, and so on. How well did the ventilation system work? This place was built in earnest, over hundreds, maybe thousands of years. Xenophon, writing in the fourth century B.C., described underground cities in Anatolia, and the tradition may go back as far as the Hittites or beyond. It seems that Kaymaklı was expanded in the seventh century A.D., when Arab armies scorched across Asia Minor and Byzantium felt the first of many Muslim tremors. Unlike the churches and monasteries, which imitated the normal architecture of their time (some even have fake masonry painted on the walls), these subterranean cities were grimly utilitarian, built for use in war. Whole generations might pass without the need to enter the dark and smelly tenements; but Anatolia was always a battleground between east and west, north and south, besides purges and civil wars within the various empires that claimed it.

Only four storeys of Kaymaklı have been opened to the public; the deepest ramifications are still choked with sediment and mystery. Nowadays, with electric light, clean air, and no inhabitants, the caves have a primal, almost Freudian fascination. These are the innards of Mother Earth. The sinuous galleries might be the burrows of giant creatures, some sort of rodent, long extinct; and it's only when you see the flights of steps, the millstones running in slots to act as doors, the wine vats and chimneys, that you remember *people* built this, scooping and hauling every cubic foot of space to the surface in small baskets. One marvels at human ingenuity in building such a refuge, and at the human terror that made it necessary.

You can still smell the fear. The guide says 60,000 could have sheltered in this city, which seems far too many, but even a tenth that number would have made it a hellish place: bawling animals and babies, the sick and dying, darkness, soot, sweat, excrement, rotting food, vermin, and an enemy prowling above, laying waste the normal, sunny life on the planet's surface, trying to find a way in, a way of poisoning the water and the air. For a moment you are thankful that such things are in the past; then you wonder if the future will be any different.

Back at Ürgüp the cliffs are draped with enormous portraits of two men: Kemal Atatürk, founder of modern Turkey, and President Evren, the republic's present leader. Atatürk, like Lenin, has fierce brows and a gaze fixed on Progress—you can almost see a capital P burning in his steel-blue eyes. Evren is avuncular but distant. The tradition of iconography hasn't died; it has become secular, and the secular has been given a touch of the divine. Torn between Europe and Asia, Jesus and Mohammed, Turkey transformed itself by an act of will only sixty years ago. Turks stopped writing their language in Arabic script and adopted the Roman alphabet; fez and veil were abolished; the solar calendar of Europe replaced the lunar cycles of the Prophet; mosques became museums; the sultan, once titular head of Islam, was overthrown. Positivism, Christianity's godless child, became the creed of the state.

President Evren has come for the gala opening of Göreme's tourist season. Suddenly we see the national costumes banned for more than half a century: orange-and-red dresses studded with sequins and silver buttons; men in britches and curious black hats that look a *bit* like fezzes. The Eastern culture, silenced like an old family scandal, has been rehabilitated as a tourist attraction. After the party is over these young dancers will go back to their university studies in engineering and commerce. The relics of Ottoman Turkey will be put back in the box. Meanwhile the nation's leaders are petitioning the European Economic Community to be allowed to join.

In the end, you see, Byzantium won.

EIGHT

Going to the Wall

After finishing my first book in 1982, I didn't return to Peru for several years. The 1980s saw the growth of a bloody guerrilla movement, *Sendero Luminoso* (Shining Path). More than 20,000 died in violence committed by both insurgents and government forces. You also heard about the odd gringo disappearing or being found dead in a remote area. I was told by friends and contacts that much of the ground I'd covered in *Cut Stones and Crossroads* was no longer safe for travel.

I got back at last in the autumn of 1988, just as the presidential election campaign was beginning to make headlines because one of the candidates was a novelist with an international reputation. I'd admired several of Mario Vargas Llosa's books, especially *Conversations in the Cathedral* and *The Green House,* but I'd always been puzzled by the way his vision of Peru seemed confined to the lowlands—to the desert coast (where Lima lies) and the Amazon frontier. One can read most of Vargas and be unaware that the Andes exist, that more than half of Peru lives there, that Peru is half Indian, speaking not Spanish but Quechua, the language of the Incas. Authors, of course, may choose whatever material they want; politicians need to be more catholic.

Andean Peru has produced its own great modern writer,

José María Arguedas (1911-69). Some of Arguedas's work, including his masterpiece, *Deep Rivers*, is available in English, but his complexity and authenticity have not made him fashionable abroad. Vargas Llosa, on the other hand, has usually been in step with literary chic outside Peru—spending much of his adult life in Paris and London. Politically, too, he has swum with the tide: a left turn in the 1950s; a sharp right for the 1980s.

My first inkling that beneath Vargas the writer lay a disturbing politician came when I read a speech he gave in 1977 to Peru's literary academy. In this he attempted the character assassination of Arguedas—who had died eight years before, by his own hand, from despair at the Peruvian condition. Vargas could not accept that Arguedas might have understood the mountain world he himself ignored. What Arguedas had portrayed so brilliantly—the discrimination and Dickensian injustice endured by indigenous Peru—was untrue, claimed Vargas Llosa. Arguedas's inspiration was not Andean reality at all, merely an unhappy childhood; his work, Vargas said, was "a beautiful lie".

During his presidential campaign, the urbane novelist successfully presented himself to the foreign press as a sensitive champion of democracy, a Latin Václav Havel. Literati and intellectuals ate from his hand as he travelled the world soliciting funds from governments and corporations. Within Peru, where he had allied himself with the small but powerful white oligarchy, his reception was rather different.

I did not go to Peru in search of Mario Vargas Llosa, but in one way or another he haunted the trip.

IT'S MY LAST NIGHT in Cusco and I still haven't been to the Wall. Now, Cusco is a city famous for walls—Inca stonework is, I think, the finest ever done—but this is *the* Wall, known in Spanish as El Muro and in Quechua, the Inca language, as Pirqa.

I follow my memories down a narrow, cobbled street so steep that it falls in steps: broken paving, the smell of drains and cooking fires burning eucalyptus wood, *wayno* songs wailing from cheap radios. Somewhere round here is what I'm looking for. I ask two Indian women chatting in a doorway. Their fringed lampshade hats are outlined by a distant light; one says, "In Cusco there are many walls, señor." Then they laugh and admit I've found it, sending me across a dark patio lit only by a spatter of stars above the sway-backed roofs. A pig grunts. I see light through cracks in a door.

On the other side of the door is a kitchen with a charcoal brazier and large blackened pots. Across the room, which is a kind of lean-to built against the Cyclopean masonry for which the place is named, are a wooden table and bench painted pale green. Men in ponchos and portly women in bowler hats are playing cards beneath a bulb that dangles from the burlap ceiling. On the table stand tall glass beakers shaped like flowerpots. Everyone looks up, surprised to see a gringo. Somebody speaks in Quechua and the others laugh.

There isn't anywhere to sit. A man staggers past me with a pail he's just lifted from the stove. In it is a feculent adobe-coloured liquid: *chicha*, the corn homebrew of the Andes. He nods towards a second room, also built against the ancient wall. There, two men in a corner are deep in conversation; at another table is a woman of about sixty with long grey braids; beside her sits a young man with a Fu Manchu moustache and a tawny thatch protruding from a scarecrow hat adorned with a paste emerald. He wears two sweaters—a red one showing through holes in the pink—and is listening to a soccer match on a tube wireless perched on a bracket just below the ceiling. He winks at me and beckons.

I sit down and order a bottled beer. It was my intention to drink some chicha, but the sight of the pail has reminded me how chicha is made: old women with bad teeth chew corn so that enzymes in their saliva will ferment it. The brew is then buried in large earthenware pots for several weeks. It is dug up, heated, and served lukewarm.

"Manolo," the young man says, extending his hand.

"What are you doing here?" he adds in Quechua, grinning at the others. I glance around vacantly, trying to think of the right word. A large hen starts pecking at my feet; several guinea-pigs (menu items) are foraging on the floor, stalked by a grey kitten with a dirty nose.

"*Reqsispa*," I say, which means, roughly, getting to know the place. This breaks the ice. The woman laughs, the chicken stops pecking me, a collie dog by the door rolls over on his back, and the owner looks in to see if we want more drinks.

"Have some chicha!" says Manolo, flashing a row of golden teeth, and I give in. Drinking in the Andes is a ritual; it's bad form to refuse. At first I took him for one of those hippies who came here years ago and never left. But no—he's a Cusco graduate student, an anthropologist studying traditional healing and religion in the cloud forest of the eastern Andes.

"It's all pure," he insists, "pure Inca!"

"Sshh. *Silencio*," hiss the others in the bar. They want to hear the football scores.

Manolo plucks a scrap of paper from the floor and draws me a map. He turns the paper over and furiously sketches diagrams of Andean cosmology. The four directions, the three levels of the world, the mountain gods, the sun and moon—everything is still there among the people he calls *Phuyu Runa*, the Cloud People.

Like many Cusqueños, he is proud not only of the ancient Incas but of the living culture descended from them; he insists we speak Quechua, even though I could follow him more easily in Spanish.

The soccer match ends and flute music fills the room. Others join us, and rounds of chicha come and go. Everyone drinks together, raising the heavy beakers with both hands. My Quechua becomes more fluent. I notice that the vessels we are drinking from are shaped exactly like the silver and gold ones used in Inca times, and this seems an epiphany, a sign that the Incas are more than ghosts. Here we are, drinking their beer, speaking their language, listening to their music, and talking about their conception of the world.

"This is the first chicha I've drunk in years," I say, adding that I've steered clear of it since the time it made me deathly ill. (I don't go into details: several days and nights of misery in a cheap hotel with no running water. *Don't leave any food in your pack*, a predecessor had scrawled on the wall above my bed. *Some large rodent just ate its way through mine.*) That was in the early seventies, when Peru was ruled by a visionary general who broke up the haciendas, made Quechua an official language, and gave speeches in it to bewildered foreign diplomats. In those days Cusco's plaza was unlit, surrounded by tiny tea-shops damp and bare as looted tombs. The nights were so clear and the city so dark that only the cold seemed to prevent your substance from evaporating into the galaxy that wheeled overhead.

Little tea-shops are gone from the city centre now, displaced by hotel lobbies and stalls full of alpaca sweaters and woolly llama toys. Nostalgia. I felt it in the streets I knew, in the smell of piss on adobe, in the guttural crunch of Quechua, in the candle-glimmer spilling from worm-eaten church doors. The old Cusco is still here, even if it has been chased to sidestreets and hillside shantytowns.

The city I remember is only a fragment of the imperial city of five centuries ago. That Cusco was capital of an empire stretching from central Chile to southern Colombia, from the coastal desert to the fringes of the Amazon. The Incas, like the Romans, ruled nearly everything they knew. "My ancestors there in the centre," wrote one who survived the Spanish conquest, "called themselves lords of the four quarters of the world. For they thought there could surely be no more world than this."

But there was. And that other world burst murderously upon them, first in the form of smallpox, then in the person of Francisco Pizarro. In November 1532, he captured the emperor Atawallpa and set in motion the events that have blighted this land. Peru became two nations, two languages, two cultures—the one austere, reverent, self-disciplined; the other baroque, impulsive, and fanatical—partners in a sour, unequal marriage that began in rape and cannot be dissolved.

"A lot of changes since the General Velasco years," I say, hoping to draw Manolo out. But he answers me with questions.

"What's new? What do you see?"

"For one thing, the sky was wrong, until today. All that smoke." I explain (in Spanish) that at this time of year, here at more than 11,000 feet, I remember a deep electric blue, even at noon. And at night a luminous powdering of stars. But a haze has dulled the Andes almost every day since I arrived a fortnight ago, fading the beige and purple hillsides, soiling the white cusp of Mount Ausangate, which rises a further 10,000 feet on Cusco's eastern horizon.

Manolo sags on his elbows and looks at me. Resignation has seeped into his dark eyes, drowning his euphoria and pride.

"The trees are burning. From Peru to Brazil. Even in the cloud forest where I work, where usually it never stops raining. The police arrested a farmer down the Urubamba valley, just last week. He set a fire to clear his field and burned the gorge right to the edge of Machu Picchu! But he's only a scapegoat. We've had years of drought, and at the same time people are moving down, down into the jungle, burning everywhere to plant their crops. And the fucking Brazilians are moving the other way, up towards Peru."

We all drink a round in silence. Then Manolo begins keening quietly in Quechua, into his beer:

Orqopi ischu kañasqay
Qasapi ischu kañasqay
Hinallaraqchus rupachkan,
Hinallaraqchus rawrachkan.

Hinalla rupariptinqa
Hinalla rawrariptinqa
Warma weqechaykiwan challaykuy,
Warma weqechaykiwan tasnuykuy.

(The grass I lit on the mountain,
The grass I burned on the peak,
How it must be burning,
How it must be blazing.

If it is still burning, girl,
If it is still blazing,
Sprinkle it with your tears,
Quench it with your sorrow.)

The woman in braids speaks up. "You know what people say, gringo? They say the United States and Russia have learned how to hide the rain for themselves, and there's nothing left for us Peruvians." Manolo fixes me with his eyes and sings again:

Ay, haykakamaraq

Wakchalla kasun
Kay Peru nasiunpi?

(Oh, for how much longer
Must we be poor
In this nation of Peru?)

"Surely you don't believe that?" I say to Manolo. "About the Russians and Americans."

"Not literally. But we've heard about global warming. The greenhouse effect. Is it not, shall we say, poetic truth?"

You don't often see a novelist reviled on public walls, but the name of Mario Vargas Llosa has been daubed angrily all over Cusco. I saw it on adobe compounds near the airport: VARGAS LLOSA, DEFENDER OF THE BANKERS! I saw it again on Inca walls in the centre. There, on grey stones fitted like gems, the insult was more direct: CUSCO HATES YOU, BOURGEOIS!

"It seems your famous writer has no honour in his own land," I remark to Manolo, when he has returned from a fit of staring into his chicha as if expecting a vision.

"Some say, *poor Vargas*, he's just a scribbler who's being manipulated by right-wingers. But not many Cusqueños think that. I went to hear him when he was here last week. I went thinking he was after the publicity, or perhaps the experience, something to write about. Who knows?" Manolo pauses for effect. "But you only have to watch him to know that here is a man who really *wants* to be president. And anyone who has that ambition in Peru today is either a fool or a demagogue—and I don't think he's stupid. Vargas is always in fashion. He was a communist when everyone was, now he's a conservative. In his books he used to attack the Lima establishment. Now he's joined it."

Writers in Latin America are expected to be on the side of the angels, not the bankers. It is easy to see why the left feels betrayed.

But perhaps some of this anger in Cusco is because of what Vargas Llosa once wrote in the *New York Times* about the Incas, who may be forgotten in Lima, the Spaniards' capital, but are remembered here: "I've never liked [them.] I've always thought that Peruvian melancholy—a notable trait in our character—was probably born under the Incas."

I quote this to the others. The woman throws up her head and laughs like a coyote. Manolo spits on the floor.

"Yes, we are sad. We are cynical. We are always pessimistic," he says drily. "In Peru we have a saying: *Se sufre pero se aprende.* One suffers but one learns. The Spanish invasion destroyed ninety per cent of our people in three generations. Don't you think that had rather more to do with it?"

I, too, had heard Mario Vargas Llosa speak in Cusco the week before. I was having supper in the Cross Keys, a *pub inglés* run by some British climbers and hikers who've made Cusco their home, when the word got out: Vargas had come from Lima and was speaking nearby, just off the small plaza the Incas used to call Happiness Square. I followed others up a narrow lane to an old stone portico with iron-studded doors. Inside was a ruinous patio with the usual whiff of human shit in the corners. About fifty people and a few dogs had come—all the party faithful that Cusco could raise.

Vargas and other dignitaries were standing underneath a sagging balcony. A forty-watt bulb illuminated their suits and some confetti sprinkled like dandruff on the novelist's head and shoulders. He looked much older than in his photos, or maybe he was suffering from *soroche*, mountain sickness caused by the thin air. He listened, head suavely cocked, to a speech of welcome in Quechua—as foreign to him, no doubt, as Welsh to Margaret Thatcher. And when he replied in Spanish, saying how delighted he was to be here in this beautiful house belonging to the Popular

Christian Party (an important member of the right-wing alliance he calls his Freedom Movement), a chorus line of frantic girls began chanting *Mario! Mario! Mario!* and jumping up and down.

Vargas spoke of freedom and democracy, sentiments that travel well in any company. But I remembered the constitutional debates of ten years ago, when the Popular Christian Party fought to deprive illiterates of the vote. *That* would have disenfranchised half of Peru.

I went back to the Cross Keys with my fellow gringos and sank some Cusqueña beer in pint mugs. The next morning I felt *soroche* myself; alcohol and altitude are a bad mixture. I found a pharmacy staffed by three men in grubby white coats who looked like Volkswagen mechanics. They fixed me up with a packet of coca teabags, some glucose tablets, and a box of Aspirin, and told me to take a siesta. (Coca leaves are legal in Peru; their extract, cocaine, is a different matter.) But I was hungry, and had a lunch of steamed trout at a restaurant on the plaza with another Inca wall beside me. Cusco is the oldest continuously inhabited city in the Americas; great chunks of the Inca capital are still in use. The anti-Vargas slogans were chalked on a grand building that once belonged to the Chosen Women, "virgins" (well, some were) who served the temples and the court. Under Christendom it holds an order of silent nuns. I was staying in a small hotel with a wall running through it like a night express, the dark trapezoidal niches—the only decoration Inca architects allowed themselves—repeated endlessly like carriage windows. To our eyes, accustomed to the aesthetics of Japan and Scandinavia, this simplicity is bold and timeless. But the Spaniards, who valued ornament over substance, found the austerity of Inca taste a chilling thing.

Cusco was badly damaged in 1536, when Manku, who succeeded Atawallpa, escaped from Spanish custody, besieged the city, and set fire to its roofs in a brave effort to dislodge the invaders. But the strong walls survived. And so the conquerors kept much of what remained, content to hack doors and windows here and there, to add columns and coats of arms, daubing the Inca stonework with stucco and whitewash to hide its silent reproach of their own shoddy constructions.

I had a table with a view of Cusco's oldest church, El Triunfo, The Triumph, built by the Spaniards to celebrate their victory over Manku's army. When Manku set fire to Cusco, most of the roofs—intricate thatches, a yard thick or more—went up in flames. But the large Inca temple in which the invaders had barricaded themselves caught briefly and went out. The Europeans came to believe that the Virgin Mary had descended from heaven and personally stamped out the blaze. Sceptical Incas didn't buy this miracle: according to them, the Spaniards sent slaves onto the roof with buckets of water.

The trout gone, I was swallowing my Aspirins with a cup of coffee when the Virgin herself appeared at the church door. She was carried aloft like an Inca queen, past my window and on through the lunch-hour traffic. Behind her came a retinue of burly women in full skirts, shawls, and bowler hats, followed in turn by a raucous, braying brass band. The Virgin wore a hot pink dress and cloak embossed with silver flowers; her cherubic plaster face smiled from under a golden crown, and at her feet, in a container like a large Victorian cake stand, was a pile of potatoes. Whatever the beginnings of this Virgin as an ally of the white invaders, she has evidently taken up the duties of her Inca counterpart, Pachamama, Mother Earth. And so here in this church celebrating the Indian defeat, the Incas' descendants bring their seed potatoes to be blessed, and for them Cusco remains what it has always been: a city of the Andean gods.

Cusco is also a city of earthquakes, a palimpsest that peels itself from time to time. In 1950 the earth moved and the monastery of Santo Domingo shook off a skin of Spanish rubble to reveal walls and rooms so fine that they seemed newly carved from living rock. Here in the ancient Golden Court, high temple of the Inca state, had sat the mummified bodies of the kings and queens who preceded Atawallpa, and above them had hung a great image of the sun, "a human countenance, looking forth from amidst innumerable rays of light ... engraved on a massive plate of gold of enormous dimensions, thickly powdered with emeralds and precious stones."

Despite the irresistible tale of the conquistador who gambled away this sun before dawn, many believe the image was hidden and never found. Little else escaped. A ton and a half of gold plates were torn from the walls for Atawallpa's vast but futile ransom. Life-size gold and silver statues of people, animals, and plants were taken from the temple gardens. All were melted down. For the Incas, who did not use money, these metals had purely religious and artistic value. A sketch made around 1600 by the Indian writer Waman Puma shows a baffled Inca asking a conquistador, *"Kay qoritachu mikhunki?* Do you *eat* this gold?" And the answer, of course, was yes.

On my last day in Cusco I went for a walk in the hills above the city, hills studded with ancient shrines.

A west wind chased away the smoke in mid-afternoon and the sky became clear as ice. It was about half past four, the time of day known in Quechua as *qhata inti*, "sloping sun", when colours intensify and the Andean landscape becomes a turbulent ocean of light and shade upon which Mount Ausangate floats like an iceberg. Cusco was hidden in its valley, but as I walked back towards the city, the Incas' greatest monument broke jaggedly through the hills—Saqsawaman, a fortress-temple with three colossal zigzag walls terraced above one another. From a distance, in this light, it resembled a shark's jaw.

As you get closer you absorb the superhuman scale of the work. The ramparts are made of bulging irregular stones with rustic surfaces but perfect joints. Cieza de León, the prince of chroniclers, observed in 1553: "Some of these stones are twelve feet wide, more than twenty high, thicker than an ox, and all so delicately seated that a coin will not fit between them.... It will last as long as the world." And a Spanish viceroy wrote to his king: "I saw the fortress that [the Incas] built ... a thing that shows clearly the work of the Devil ... for it seems impossible that it could have been made by the strength and skill of man."

At the top of Saqsawaman once stood three towers with windows overlooking the city. These were of smaller stones, taken long ago for Spanish walls, but from their foundations you can still look down into Cusco's plaza five hundred feet below. Today, the rainbow flag of the Incas flaps peacefully beside the red and white flag of Peru, and the only blood is the sunset on the tiles. But it was down there that Manku's son, Tupa Amaru, was beheaded in 1572, ending the first Inca resistance. And it was there that a second Tupa Amaru—great-great-great grandson of the first—was drawn, quartered, and beheaded in 1781 for trying to restore Inca rule.

After that the native aristocracy, who had survived two and a half centuries, were broken. Many were killed or deported; all lost their titles. Quechua language and culture were officially (but ineffectually) banned. Only forty years later came independence from Spain, usurped by white Peruvians, the privileged minority that Vargas Llosa represents. Today the Inca royalty exist only in myth. But myths have power. Indians throughout the central Andes believe that their sovereign's head, cut off by the Spaniards, is growing a new body in its grave, and when the process is complete he will return from the underworld to reclaim Peru. Some have projected their hopes onto the Shining Path guerrillas, who are strong in many parts of the country, though not in Cusco. Whether that ruthless and enigmatic movement really has anything to offer the Indians remains to be seen.

In twilight Saqsawaman seemed more a geological phenomenon than a building, and it was an eerie thing to walk below the bulbous, alien walls. Soon it got dark and I descended into the labyrinth of cobbled streets that fall in steps towards the city centre. A radio was playing a *wayno* tune.

It's high time for a glass of chicha, if I can find the Wall.

NINE

Peru Is Not a Novel

When I told George Galt of *Saturday Night* that I was going back to Peru—a country he himself had visited—he agreed to take a travel piece. "I don't really care where you go," he said expansively, "as long as it's somewhere you haven't been before." I could see the literary point of this, but it was a tall order given that half the country had fallen under Shining Path control. Then I thought of Tarma.

Tarma had stuck in my mind ever since I'd read George Woodcock's wonderful *Incas and Other Men*, first published in 1959. I'd never been there, and it still seemed possible to go. According to the map, it could be reached by a paved road running east over the Andes from Lima. Paved roads, I reckoned, were probably well patrolled. I rented a Volkswagen beetle and set off.

It turned out that the map had outlived much of the paving, and in various tricky spots in the mountains where the view was splendid there were red notices saying *NO PARE: ORDEN DE DISPARAR*. At high altitude one's brain functions poorly. I got out and took a picture beside one of these signs before I realized what it said: *NO STOPPING: ORDERS TO SHOOT*. Luckily the road wasn't as thoroughly patrolled as I'd thought.

MANY YEARS LATER, as they haul me before the firing squad, I'll remember when the Tarma hotel barman discovered ice. He reached deep into his old Philco fridge and retrieved a cube triumphantly, like a man cheating a broody hen. Until then I'd been drinking Courvoisier, which we pronounced in the Spanish way to rhyme with "poor boy's ear". I asked if he knew anything about the Virgin of the Biplane and he shook his head: "Here we have only Our Lord of Muruhuay."

I explained. Weeks before, in the old Inca capital of Cusco, a breathless traveller had told me about this Virgin. "There's a shrine built over a rock and a spring," she'd said, "and some ruins that are at least a thousand years old, and a big blue biplane perched on top of them." This I had to see. There were also other reasons for coming to Tarma: 1) I'd never been; 2) it was the birthplace of General Manuel Odría, tyrant of Peru in the 1950s, and he'd showered the small Andean city with grandiose monuments; 3) Mario Vargas Llosa had written at length about the Odría years and had partly set *The Real Life of Alejandro Mayta*—his only novel to venture into the Andes—in the nearby city of Jauja. Among the nasty slogans the left had greeted Vargas with in Cusco had been *EL PERU NO ES UNA NOVELA—PERU IS NOT A NOVEL.* I had a novel of my own to write and I hoped it wasn't true.

I'd felt the late dictator's presence long before reaching Tarma. After climbing from Lima (at sea-level) to 16,000 feet in less than sixty miles and crossing one of the highest passes in the world, after jolting for hours at walking speed over a road surfaced with stones the size of baked potatoes, my VW purred like a cat when a strip of black tarmac suddenly appeared. Odría was still in power and this road was brand-new when George and Inge Woodcock came here in 1956—the best road, they were told, in all Peru, except for those of the Incas.

I passed the mines and smelters of La Oroya and climbed up onto the high plateau behind a smoking truck whose bumper said in Gothic lettering *Soy Feo Pero Fiel*—I'm Ugly but True. I overtook him and sped across some of the baldest scenery in the Andes, the limestone spine of the Americas, scraped and scarred by the glaciers of the Ice Age. Golden bunchgrass blackened here and there by fires, snow like ash on the uplands, a weak, red sun falling behind me, and not a tree in sight. This is a land where sorcerers are chosen by a lightning strike to the body, and the man standing at the roadside a mile ahead seemed a likely candidate. I gave him a lift.

He was a schoolmaster, wrapped in melancholy and a brown scarf that clung like Velcro to the stubble on his chin. His name was Alejandro and he was on the left. "All this," he said, lifting his hand to the thin grasslands and the thin sheep wandering like insects, "belongs to a co-operative!" And he spoke affectionately of Juan Velasco, a rather different general who had ruled Peru in the early seventies and broken the big families and foreign corporations. Alejandro was disillusioned with the reigning APRA social democrats, who had swept to power on a tide of hope and were now floundering in a wrack of failed policies and foiled expectations. "If the United Left wins the next election—and I think they will—there'll be a coup from the right. And then it will be between the army and *Sendero*."

The Shining Path guerrillas inhabit these desolate mountains like the shades of the Incas. You never see them but you see what they have done: broken bridges, burnt police posts, manic slogans. They are the last true Maoists in the world; they hate Lima and admire Pol Pot. Their leader, Presidente Gonzalo, is the "Fourth Sword" of Marxism (after Marx, Lenin, and Mao), and the peasants sometimes call him, in the Inca language, Puka

Inti—"Red Sun"—a name evoking both his political hue and the Indians' hope for a messianic return of their ancient solar kings. *Sendero*'s revolution was now in a latent phase, waiting for the collapse of the government, which would mean the collapse of electoral democracy. All options had been tried: the old right, the old left; the new right, the new left. All had failed.

What about Vargas Llosa? I asked. No one was going to vote for him, Alejandro said. His way was the way of the bankers and the rich whites, and Peru had had enough of all that. And besides, nobody in Peru knew his books—half the people couldn't read and the rest couldn't afford to buy them.

We left the huge sky of the plateau for wrinkled ravines and green terraces built by the Incas. General Odría's road became a chain of hairpins and began to show its age. Schoolchildren were walking up from the city centre to adobe barrios on the hillsides; naked bulbs flickered in tiny shops and bars. We passed the General Odría Park, the General Odría Playground, the General Odría Welfare Building, and the General Odría School. Alejandro got out at the General Odría Market. After that I went to the Hotel de Turistas, opened by General Odría in 1954.

It has since suffered badly from falling stars. When new it must have had four or five; the plaque by the door laid claim to three; and in the Lima head office, where I'd booked, it sat forlornly at the bottom of the list of government hotels with two. It was a cross between an Alpine lodge and a barracks, with gatehouses and about a hundred rooms. When the Woodcocks stayed here there had been tennis courts, a private zoo, and a view of open countryside. At dusk it was possible to keep these illusions, but the morning sun revealed dry fountains, dead rosebushes, and sheep grazing on weeds beside an empty swimming pool. The tennis courts had reverted to pasture, and the view from my window was hidden by adobe huts. The "zoo" held six chickens and a pig.

Evening. I took another look at my dinner and the blowfly was still there. The fly and I were the restaurant's only occupants, apart from a waiter and a large Alsatian dog who strutted confidently out of the kitchen from time to time as if he were the *maître d'*. The room was square and tall, with a hundred chairs and twenty-five pink tablecloths stained as subtly and indelibly as the Shroud of Turin. I returned to the bar and drank another cognac. Odría's hotel was a time machine stuck in 1954 and nobody else was aboard. No one sat at the red formica tables, no one flicked ash in the brown glass ashtrays. I lit a cigar and thought about a man I'd met at a posh bar in Lima two days before. He seemed to fit in here, in this empty hotel built by the old general. I bought him a poor boy's ear and helped him drink it.

Jorge, call me Georgie, was an Anglo-Peruvian oligarch whose family had got rich with General Odría. He'd lost his estates under General Velasco and later had them returned. Now he was growing flowers for North American weddings and funerals. He didn't consider this a frivolous use of land in a country that no longer feeds itself. "I give the Indians jobs, I build a school for their children, a clinic for their wives, and people like you tell me I'm an exploiter.

"Peru is the pits!" he added after a silence, accepting my cigar and sniffing it with the suspicion of one accustomed to the best. "Peru will be the next Cuba—wait and see! There are hundreds of Russians already here. We have some living at the end of our street. They speak excellent Spanish. They speak perfect English like you and me. They're blond. You can't tell them from Americans!"

"How do you know they're not Americans?"

"I know," he said mysteriously. He sniffed again at the cigar.

"Havana tobacco, rolled in Montreal," I said, to reassure him.

"I've met Fidel," he said. "I've met García, I've met Pinochet, I've met them all. And you know what?" He lit the cigar, took a long drag, and stubbed it out in disgust. He looked me in the eye, raised his right hand, and stabbed his fingers at the ceiling: "Pinochet is my god!"

"He killed and tortured thousands...."

"He knew what to do with communists! You cut off their balls and drop them out of helicopters—it's the only way."

Next morning I walked down to the plaza. Tarma likes to call itself the "Pearl of the Andes" but is really nothing special. The streets are very narrow, the concrete paving cracked and muddy. None of the buildings seems more than a century old, and everything is dominated by the heavy piles of the patriarch. In Tarma it will always be 1954.

Odría's cathedral is a pseudo-Colonial nonentity, stuccoed beige and streaked where people piss against it regularly. (Not a political statement; it happens all over Peru.) There was a sign—SHOW SOME CULTURE, DON'T FOUL YOUR CATHEDRAL—and an overpowering reek. A plaque beside the door reminded worshippers of the building's inauguration by General Odría, "Constitutional President of the Republic". ("Constitutional" was a nice touch: he won a rigged election two years after his *coup d'état.*) The general was still here, in a sarcophagus near the high altar. It had a glass front, but the corpse was hidden by a lace screen. Another plaque: *Por mi patria doy la vida, por Tarma mi corazón*—I give my life for my country, and for Tarma my heart. Was it genuine, his affection? He never came back to live. He idled in a Lima mansion from the day he stepped down in 1956 until his death eighteen years later. His generosity to Tarma was merely the display of a local boy made good. As one Peruvian remarked drily to the Woodcocks: "The moral is that each town in Peru should provide a president in its turn."

Odría has just stepped down when Alejandro Mayta, Vargas Llosa's protagonist, begins dreaming of revolution. He's from Lima, an urban creature of filthy cafés, verminous roominghouses, and a small garage where he helps to edit the Trotskyist *Workers Voice.* He smokes Inca brand cigarettes—the cheapest ones. His dreams might have remained just that, as is usual with Trots, but in Lima he meets Lieutenant Vallejos, an army officer with ideals of radical change. The lieutenant tells Mayta that the real Peru is up here in the Andes where the spirit of the Incas still lives, that here—not in the capital—will revolution be made. The lieutenant brings Mayta to Jauja, where they take over the barracks, rob a bank, and head into the mountains with money and weapons for the Indians. But they forget to cut the telegraph, and are quickly captured. Like most others in Peru, the revolution is a pathetic and ridiculous *fracaso.*

The exception is *Sendero,* the Shining Path, which Peruvians like to say is the only thing in the country that works. The narrator of Vargas's book—a novelist piecing together the story of Mayta thirty years later—inhabits a Peru of the near future. The guerrillas are closing in, bombs explode daily in the cities, every conversation takes place in the shadow of informers and death squads. If the novelist in the book is Vargas himself, and if this is his vision of Peru, why does he want so much to be the next *presidente*? Could he be hoping that Peru is not a novel?

On General Odría Avenue I drove out of Tarma. I passed Acobamba and a great sign by the road: TO OUR BENEFACTOR, GENERAL ODRIA. In the green mountains to the east, where Mayta and Vallejos were captured in the novel, a real Indian leader who took the royal name of Atawallpa had waged a guerrilla war against the Spaniards for nearly twenty years in the mid-eighteenth century. He was never defeated, but his rebellion died when a traitor killed him in 1761.

I turned left down a dirt road flanked with magueys and crumbling stone walls. Thirty minutes later I reached the home of the miraculous Señor de Muruhuay. A brass band was playing *wayno* tunes in front of a small bar when I arrived, and several couples were dancing. I bought some beer and drank it with the musicians; we traded Quechua songs, but they could hardly understand my Cusco dialect here—hundreds of miles from the ancient capital—nor I theirs.

Was there a Virgin? I asked. No, they said, only the Señor. What about an aeroplane? They pointed to a hill covered in flowering shrubs and eucalyptus trees. I climbed an ornamental stairway with mottos painted on the rocks beside it. GOD AND NATURE ARE SYNONYMOUS, said one, which seemed very Andean; another was more Confucian: FOR THE LAZY MAN, EVERYTHING IS DIFFICULT. Beyond were ancient walls of Inca or pre-Inca date, and above, perched on a cairn, sat the biplane. It had a blue fuselage and silver wings. Birds had pecked and torn its canvas, and the wind was soughing in its struts and stays.

The Inca royalty were sky worshippers, claiming descent from sun and moon, but the ordinary folk over whom they ruled were mainly animists, worshipping Mother Earth and Wiraqocha, the water deity who made her fertile. After the Spaniards came, bringing their god nailed to a piece of wood, Wiraqocha changed his name to Our Lord and made countless appearances at the rocks and springs where he had always been revered. And so it was, during a smallpox plague about two hundred years ago, that waters from a spring beneath a crag at Muruhuay were found to have healing powers. Years later, a painting of Christ crucified appeared on the rock overnight. This portrait, it was said, had no earthly origin, and it became known as the Señor. A rustic chapel was built around Him; pilgrims began to come in thousands from all over Peru; and eventually the Bishop of Tarma opened a vast modern sanctuary of reinforced concrete with a salient tower containing three electric bells. A local pilot added the biplane, thus restoring, in his own way, worship of the sky.

I went in to see the Señor. He was protected by a sheet of glass and surrounded by a silver frame. Dozens of candles burned in front of Him; worshippers attended in pews, or on their knees. The mountain air was thick with incense, wax, and a calm yet desperate piety. One by one the faithful shuffled past the Lord, touching the glass and stuffing paper money into a collection box as they prayed:

Oh, Señor de Muruhuay,
May there be neither
Rich nor poor,
Nor borders,
Nor races,
Nor flags...
Enlighten all Peruvians,
That together we may save Peru.

And in their eyes upcast, and in the downcast eyes of the miraculous Señor, I saw that Peru was not a novel; it was a prayer.

TEN

Crossroads

Except when travelling for books and articles, I've never kept a journal. I've never even wanted very much to keep one. I'm too lazy, and my memory, though fallible, is good enough that I rely on it to stow the past. Be that as it may, one of the reasons I began my first book was the fear that memory might fade. Even if the book was never published, it could at least become the diary I hadn't written.

When *Cut Stones and Crossroads* was accepted for publication, it could no longer fill that role. For in a successful travel book or article—even one that follows the "fake diary" form, such as Robert Byron's *Road to Oxiana*—what stays out is as important as what goes in. A complete account of one's travels would be as disastrous as an exhaustive showing of one's holiday slides. Much of what you leave out is dross, but sometimes, for reasons of structure or space, you have to discard good ore.

One day Alberto Manguel told me he was guest-editing Bloomsbury's literary annual, *Soho Square III*, and would like me to contribute. "I want something rough," he said, a hint of mischief in his normally august expression. "Something you couldn't get published anywhere else." He would not elaborate on this odd request—Manguel is a great literary pack-rat, and apparently he asked more or less the same of other contributors. Certainly he did of Julian Barnes, whom I rang up once on Alberto's behalf when I was in London. "Something rough," Barnes said wryly. "That doesn't make it any easier, does it?"

Barnes was right, but I persevered in my *bricolage.* Alberto obviously wanted the feel of raw material—notes, jottings, sketches from the road. It was a chance to rescue fragments from earlier trips, random marginalia, recent Peruvian material—things that held the imagination or stood out in memory but had never found a home in print. Later, when the galleys came for checking, Alberto let slip that he'd been widely ignored. "You," he said, "were one of the few who did what I asked."

Petén, Guatemala, 1985

ARMY ROADBLOCKS every twenty miles or so. I've been searched three times. I write these notes in my worst handwriting, so nobody can read them. "Even paranoids have enemies," as Rod used to say. It was a joke then.

"Assassination is the sincerest form of flattery." – Suzanne Ruta

Tikal

One hundred per cent humidity, dripping trees, mist hanging like smoke in the branches, rasp of a toucan, a smell of wild allspice.

Dinner was chop suey *generis.* The waiter (black bowtie, white shirt, faded charcoal trousers, elderly) had a collapsed look, like a badly stuffed cushion. Someone said, "You could regard being President of the United States as the perfect crime."

Howler monkeys woke me twice last night—a sound like rutting camels, hungry lions, fighting dogs. Monkeys, the Maya believe, are descendants of an earlier race of man which the gods judged imperfect and banished to the forest. The howler is also patron of writing: what a voice!

Tarma, Peru, 1988. Don Julio

The power fails and the stars come out over Tarma (population 28,933; altitude 10,000 feet). I remember the astronomer and go to see him. Don Julio Rivera is the owner of the Hostal Central, a small hotel with no stars.

He's resting on a cot in his office, hoping for lodgers to turn up.

"So you've come to see my telescope?" (A tweed cap, a stoop, twinkling expression—like a garden gnome dressed as Sid James.) "First I'll show you *mi telescopio de cartón*—my cardboard telescope!" He goes over to a desk piled three feet high with exercise books. On top of the books is a cardboard disk with degrees and hours marked on its circumference. It has an arrow pivoted in the middle like the hand of a toy clock.

"Let us observe Jupiter and Mars!"

Don Julio chooses a dog-eared notebook and opens it. On each page are columns of figures and ancient astronomical symbols for the planets and zodiac. "People think I'm crazy, or a wizard, or both. But let me convince you." He aims his cardboard "telescope" at a spot on the wall which he says is north; he tilts it to conform with Tarma's latitude and the time of year; he moves the arrow until it rests on a number given in his tables. "There! At exactly 9:17 p.m. Jupiter will rise from behind that hill in the east."

He points through the window to a small nub on the mountain silhouette. "Now let us go to the observatory and see if I'm crazy or not."

Across a dark patio and up several flights of stairs. Rooms leading off balconies, candles glowing behind thin curtains. At last we come out on the roof and there, against the dome of heaven, is a darker dome—a mushroom shape about twenty feet high. Don Julio chuckles and unlocks a metal door. The power comes on again, revealing a round space with three large sofas against the walls. "I built it to seat fifteen," he says, as if seating capacity was the main consideration in its design. When he removes the canvas cover from his (real) telescope I see that this is indeed the case—the instrument is a four-inch refractor, newer but no bigger than the one I take out occasionally on my lawn. It looks lost in here, like a shotgun in the turret of a battleship.

"You do a lot of entertaining...?"

"One or two people come up from time to time. But nobody is serious. Even though this is the only observatory in Peru!"

"Surely the university in Lima...?"

"I went to see them once, to show them my system, my telescope of cardboard! They have nothing!" He laughs wistfully. "They even gave me this." From a box he produces a twelve-inch disk of glass, concave on one side, its reflective silvering as tarnished as a forgotten christening spoon. This was once the eye of a Newtonian reflector on a mountain in Chile. When it became obsolete the Chileans gave it to Peru. Peru gave it to Don Julio. One day he plans to build a better telescope, but he is old now, with no one to help. Besides, there's another problem. "You can't get mirrors resilvered here. I'd have to send it to Buenos Aires. Or New York. Imagine the difficulties! Imagine the cost!" He puts away the glass mirror, sadly, like an old maid repacking her trousseau. He rests a hand on the refractor.

"What I'd really like is another like this, only bigger, say six-inch aperture. Perhaps a society in your country has such an instrument they no longer use. We could make an exchange—their telescope, my observatory. They could come here to watch the southern skies. Would you mention it when you get home?"

At exactly 9:17 p.m. we look east towards the mountain.

Jupiter rises.

Tabloid headline: STATUE OF ELVIS FOUND ON MARS

Tarma, Peru. Euhemerism

A newspaper cutting, very yellow—about 1970 to judge from the value of the *sol.* My translation (abridged):

Traffic in Human Flesh in Peru
They Were Hunting Men and Women to Sell As Beef

> *A traffic in human flesh has just been uncovered by Tarma police, in the central Andean region, according to information revealed today. Twenty-six people were attacked in lonely parts of the departments of Cusco, Ayacucho, and Huancayo in order to supply carcasses to an individual identified only as "The Gringo"....*
>
> *Isaac Martínez and his brother Pedro explained how they killed persons they found alone in the Andes. Afterwards they removed the limbs, as "The Gringo" was interested only in torsos. These were gathered and delivered to Lima in a van by one known as "The Fox".*
>
> *The Martínez brothers revealed the prices they charged, which were determined by weight: a woman eight months pregnant was valued at 15,000 soles (a little more than 300 dollars), fat men fetched 8,000 soles, and thin ones 5,000....*
>
> *At first it was believed that the criminals were* pishtacos,

> *legendary brigands or wizards of the Andes, who attack men and women in lonely spots....*

Lima, 1982

Juan Ossio, professor of anthropology, tells me that Indians believe the fat taken by *pishtacos* is used by Max Factor for making cosmetics. Poetic truth: who wears cosmetics in Peru? Not Indians, but the wives of those who get rich from Indian sweat. At the time of the Conquest, Indians believed that the Spaniards took their fat for curing a great sickness in Spain. Literal truth: "We dressed our wounds with the fat from a stout Indian whom we had killed and cut open," wrote Bernal Díaz, who fought in Mexico with Cortés.

In Bolivia, perhaps they have Klaus Barbie dolls.

Lima, 1988

Two sheep, one alpaca, one llama, eating the grass behind Pizarro Palace, where lives the *presidente.* Only the sheep look happy in the thick air of a coastal winter. No sunshine and no rain for months, but plenty of drizzle and fog. A bubble of visibility moves with me through the grey. Police keep people from the palace walls—to stop them tossing bombs.

A young man seated at a kitchen table in a filthy room with rain streaming down uncurtained windows. A kettle is boiling away on the stove. The young man is plunging a hypodermic needle into his arm. Paint in oils, entitle: *Rain, Steam, and Speed.*

Miraflores, Lima

Clifftop near the roundabout with Wolfie's Grill. In Vargas Llosa's

Historia de Mayta, the narrator (V. Ll. himself, of course) describes how the cliffs behind his wealthy suburb—a suburb like this—are strewn with rubbish that nobody ever takes away. It's true. Here's a little park, some threadbare grass still damp from the gardener's hose, and dusty magueys that get watered much less often. The desert above and the beach below are the same colour: tan. The sea is lead. A tan dog with foxy ears, elegant in its leanness, picks through a picnic lunch.

Lovers: some standing, some prone; in motionless clinches, unaware of me, of the dog, of apartment windows watching them; lovers wreathed in smoke rising from a rubbish pile on the beach. Burning rubbish smells the same all over the world, and yet this is peculiarly Lima's smell: singed cans, shit, and rancid cooking oil: in hotel towels, in mattresses, on banknotes, in people's hair, in my hair.

A phallic lighthouse, striped black and white like a sock, its lens sweeping, stabs into a thousand living rooms and my two eyes. Below the apartments, in a gravel ravine, there's an infestation of squatters' shacks: a wrinkle of poverty on the fat cheeks of Miraflores. Homes of driftwood and plastic and old doors and zinc sheets held down with stones and hope. A baby wails, a radio wanders on and off the station (Afro-Andean *chicha* tunes). Breakers roll in from the Pacific fog. Headlands and tall buildings dissolve into the overcast.

There again, on the wall of Wolfie's Grill, is that message for Vargas Llosa: *PERU IS NOT A NOVEL.*

ELEVEN

Invading Grenada

Today, after Panama and the Gulf War, the American invasion of Grenada has been all but forgotten, though it was a dress rehearsal for both of those. I remember following the news in 1983: first Ronald Reagan's media campaign to vilify and demonize Maurice Bishop; then the coup by Grenadian hardliners apparently much further to the left; and finally their murder of Bishop, which provided the occasion for the United States to do what it had been poised to do for months—to invade and "restore order". As in Panama, restoration of order caused far more death and damage than the evils it was supposed to correct. I remember the first reports of the invasion—heavily massaged reports—and the radio playing Phil Ochs:

And the eyes of the dead are turning every head...
The Marines have landed on the shores of Santo Domingo....

"Invading Grenada", written four years later, is more about travel than politics. But I must have struck some sort of balance, for I received two angry letters. One attacked me for being soft on communism; the other for playing down the Americans' crimes.

POINT SALINES AIRPORT, once considered a threat to the free world, has one runway and its fuel tanks are exposed conspicuously on a knoll. Polished floors pick up the sound of your shoes and send it echoing from the glass of the empty shops across the customs hall. The Marines have left, but the flood of tourists expected to follow the 1983 "rescue" from Marxism has never materialized. The island aches for visitors, the immigration officers are friendly, the taxi driver shakes your hand. His name is Welcome Cummings.

Photographer Zoran Milic and I arrived on one day's notice, but the choice of places to stay was almost unlimited. If we'd wanted satellite TV and paper seals across the toilet bowls we could have chosen the Ramada Renaissance, thoroughly sanitized since U.S. troops kicked in the doors and hauled suspicious-looking foreigners from their beds. There was the Balisier, not far from the mental hospital the Americans bombed; or the Spice Island Inn on Grand Anse beach, the Calabash on Prickly Bay, and a little place called No Problem Apartments, all ticking over on half a dozen guests apiece. But the place I wanted wasn't available: the old Ross Point Inn had a shield over the gate and a Stars and Stripes on its flagpole—a temporary occupation had become permanent and it was now the American embassy.

We checked into the Spice Island and were given a welcoming rum punch that would nobble a racehorse. Zoran's room had crabs, but they were bona fide crustaceans the size of hamburgers. White sand stretched for miles in each direction; surf crashed and seethed a few steps from my door. It was dark by seven p.m., and the cicadas sounded like a hundred squeaky wheels.

The rental car had squeaky wheels, and a warning never to exceed twenty-five miles per hour. It was good advice; in Grenada the motorist is never bored. It was a rare thing to reach top gear and whistle past banana trees and tethered goats and minibuses that threw reggae like a beating when they jousted with you for the best course between potholes and pedestrians. The island—only twenty miles long, thrown up by volcanoes, irrepressibly fertile, and home to a hundred thousand people—seems many times its actual size. Narrow roads scribble around it like a faded script. The coasts have been nibbled and chewed into countless bluffs and more than forty beaches by the warm bite of the Caribbean. Something new around each bend: a straggling village, a great stone church, a dog asleep in the road, a view down a precipice to a bay, a reef, bottle-green headlands ploughing the turquoise sea.

Grenada has a long history of invasion, migration, and bravura. The Arawaks were followed by the Caribs; the French by the British. Columbus sailed past in 1498, still thinking he was in Asia; within two centuries the island was filled with African slaves. It's the birthplace of the Haitian king Henri Christophe and the calypso singer Mighty Sparrow. Somehow a marble bathtub belonging to Napoleon's Josephine ended up in the national museum. Eric Gairy, the wild and wily politician who dominated Grenada until 1979, made himself and his country famous by addressing the United Nations on the subject of flying saucers.

I began with the Caribs. Nowadays there's little left of them but their name on a local beer. Near a village called Hermitage a sign at the roadside announces the Carib Stone. There at the bottom of a ravine lies a great boulder covered in pictographs, some abstract, others showing the face of a god wearing an ornate headdress. This is sometimes said to be the work of Arawaks, a supposedly gentle, cultured people displaced by both Caribs and Columbus; but whatever the truth, the scene of the Caribs' own demise isn't far away. At the northern tip of Grenada is the town of Sauteurs, named for a cliff where the Indians jumped to their deaths rather than surrender to the French in 1652. Two old brick churches, one Catholic, the other Anglican, are built near the edge. I searched among overgrown graves for a view of the precipice, but the sky darkened to slate, and rain blew in across the sea. I sheltered in St Patrick's, and climbed up the bell tower as far as I dared. Termites had weakened the wooden stairs, and my sandals slithered on loose plaster and wet bat droppings. The town was visible through a small window, muted by lacy curtains of rain. Red and blue and yellow houses, rusty roofs, the raging orange of the flame trees—all were softened and doused until this tropical headland seemed like a Scottish coast and it was quite impossible to visualize the heroic death of those people who gave the Caribbean its name and the English language (rightly or wrongly) the word *cannibal.* Here they had left no names: the gravestones told a different history, of slavery and a taste for grandiose appellations—Augustus Robinson, Festus Braveboy, Dorcas Springle—redolent of Twain and reggae albums.

We lunched at Betty Mascoll's plantation house, Morne Fendue, built by her father early in this century. It took some time to find. There are few signs in Grenada, and Grenadians have a habit of telling you to "go straight op, bendin' no angles" on roads as crooked as intestines. The farmhouse is not very different from those of the same age in Canada, except that the stone walls are mortared with lime and molasses, and surrounded by flamboyants, poinsettia trees, and cascades of bougainvillaea. Mrs. Mascoll was away; we were admitted by Frances, her housekeeper, who serves a stiff punch in a tumbler and leaves you in the drawing-room with ghosts and relics of the years. Family photographs reaching back to Victorian times sat on the grand piano like passengers in steamer chairs. Termites had left their trails on the lime-green walls; brown spots of decay had crept into framed lithographs of Gothic buildings and Marie Antoinette. Above an Edwardian chaise-longue was a commendation from Elizabeth II to Mrs. Mascoll, MBE, for volunteer work, dated 1959, and a picture of the young queen dining in this room. Willow-pattern plates hung below a heavy plaster cornice. Every shelf, windowsill, and mahogany cabinet was laden with ornaments. I stared, overwhelmed by the dusty intricacy of the figurines. Suddenly one of them would start and run up the curtains, and only then could the eye distinguish a living gecko from a lifeless ivory.

The wind shook the palms outside and rattled the etched glass in the verandah doors and transom windows. Another rum punch, showered with nutmeg. Grenada is often called the Spice Isle. Plantations such as this grew rich on bay leaves, cinnamon, nutmeg and mace, which thrive in the volcanic soil. The meal began with soup made from *callaloo* (a Grenadian improvement on spinach); this was followed by fried bananas and "pepper-pot", a meat and cassava stew with toasted spices—delicious. Frances produced a small jar of homemade sauce. "Dis one de hot one," she said. "I show you how moch." She took a tiny spatula and metered it out like a dangerous substance, and so it was.

Grenada's capital, St. George's, occupies a natural setting as delightful in its way as that of Río. The town of 8,000 hugs two natural harbours formed by volcanic craters, and the houses climb into the steep surrounding hills with the colour and tenacity of tropical plants. It has a sturdier, more permanent look than the run of Britain's tropical outposts. Some of the buildings date to the eighteenth century, many to the nineteenth. Most are brick or stone with roofs tiled in fishscale patterns. Grenada's French Catholicism, and Anglican efforts to supplant it, have left a generous collection of spires and religious schools. The physical struggles of the same powers produced two large forts and several smaller strongholds. From a distance, St. George's might be Mediterranean, but then you notice the inhabitants—almost all of African descent—the flame trees and frangipani, the palms, vines, and impossibly wild vegetation occupying any space not claimed and constantly reclaimed by man.

I'd been told that the best view could be had from a South American ambassador's residence at the top of a hill. But which hill? Several winding strips of asphalt ascended invitingly at rakish gradients. We followed one to a mansion guarded by three mastiffs. This had to be the place—important South Americans always have fierce dogs. The mastiffs barked and tried their teeth on the tyres. A security guard emerged from a gatehouse. I knew what to say: "I'm expected for lunch by General Morales." (There's always a General Morales.) The guard looked puzzled. "Dis de doctor's house," he said, naming one of the teachers at the medical school. During our conversation the dogs calmed down and I lowered my window. The guard waved us on our way and went inside; I pulled in my elbow just as a pair of jaws closed on the air where it had been.

We tried another hill and arrived at Fort Frederick, a massy piece of colonial architecture with stone bastions, archways, an echoing cistern, and a network of rock-hewn tunnels. Bougainvillaea climbed up its walls, and on the summit stood a TV antenna and the rusty skeleton of an illuminated steel cross erected by Prime Minister Gairy many years before. For a few days in October 1983 this was a base for the hard-line Marxist conspirators who overthrew Maurice Bishop's socialist regime. Now they await appeals against their death sentences in the grim stone prison on Richmond Hill, visible between here and the sea. Beyond that, presiding over the lower town, stands Fort George, built by the French as Fort Royal in 1705, today the Grenadian police headquarters. There, against a wall with a basketball hoop, Maurice Bishop and his colleagues were shot by firing squad.

The landscape was full of sinister reminders of the past, of Gairy's arrogance, Bishop's idealism, the bloody putsch, Reagan's much bloodier invasion. We went up to the mental hospital destroyed by U.S. bombs. (The Americans later claimed they mistook it for Fort Frederick.) It was obviously off limits, but we unwired the gate and went in. Rows of thick-walled, barred cells stood roofless to the sun. Grass had grown up through cracked courtyards, hiding shattered glass and tiles. Only a few years before it been filled with schizophrenics, depressives, and doctors in white coats. Already it looked like the ruins of a penal colony from a century ago.

A watchman appeared, preceded by a gust of rum. He was a large, muscular character with a bleeding wound across his forehead and a cutlass in his hand. Had we not been where we were, I'd have said he was auditioning for the role of a Barbary pirate.

"Wha' you tink you doin'?" he raged. "You lookin' for get youself in jeel, maan! Two bullet in de head!" It was a dodgy moment but I managed to pacify him with a technique known in Peru as the *tarjetazo*. This involves producing a business card of someone important, or at least a card that looks important. I gave him one I'd pocketed idly at the tourist office—it had an impressive Grenadian shield and some florid script—and while he was squinting at it we drove smartly away.

I thought about his question. What *were* we doing? Being a political tourist was a bit like being a sex tourist: it had an alluring *frisson* but it made you feel shabby. Yet it wasn't possible to avoid politics in Grenada: everyone had his view and version of events, and they were always different. You felt the bewilderment and resentment of the ordinary Grenadians. They knew their country had been buffeted by international forces but they weren't sure whom to blame. Young men called out things like "White Mafia!" and "CIA!" as you walked past; a Rasta took Zoran for a Russian spy. Long before the split in Maurice Bishop's party that led to his death, the Americans had waged a relentless campaign of rhetoric and vilification against his "revolutionary government", which had deposed Gairy (without violence) in 1979. Everyone I spoke to agreed that Bishop had been popular, and many were genuinely grateful for the American overthrow of his killers. But what had really happened? Was the 1983 coup merely an internal rift, or had the CIA been behind it, or the KGB, or both? No one knows. Or those who know aren't saying.

In St. George's market a young ayatollah with dreadlocks chanted, "Reagan's a devil!" into my tape recorder. "Who you wid, maan—NBC, CBS, CIA?" I said I was from Canada. "Canadian aalright, maan. You a good fella. American government wicked, maan. *Satanic!* Dey invade me land!" He raised his left fist and shook it in the air.

I spoke to local pundits: their estimates of anti-American feeling among the Grenadian people ran anywhere from 5 to 50 per cent. Over dinner one night, a hotel owner railed against "those damn communist university professors" who used to stay at his place. He thanked "Uncle Sam" and pleaded for a few more million Yankee dollars. In a suburb of St. George's a steel band hall was covered with graffiti saying: THANK GOD FOR U.S. AND CARIBBEAN HEROES OF FREEDOM! KGB BEHAVE! It was signed *Graduate from the Ghetto.* On a headland between the yacht basin and the sea stand the ruins of Bishop's offices, a burnt-out concrete shell surrounded by flamboyants and oleanders. Vegetation is already beginning to close over the wounds, and a dozen squatters have moved into rooms missed by the bombs, but the gaunt pile seems a reminder and a warning, more eloquent than any words, of the pleasure of Uncle Sam.

Every hotel has calypso piped into every room; I wanted to hear it on the hoof. Someone told me that the Mighty Sparrow himself would be appearing on Saturday night in a village called Birch Grove. Born in the town of Grand Roy, Sparrow and his parents had left Grenada for Trinidad (a land of opportunity for many Grenadians) when he was one. It sounded about as likely as finding Mick Jagger in a Clapham pub, but I've been a fan of the Sparrow for years and wasn't about to let the possibility slip. The drive to Birch Grove took me up into clouds that seemed to hang permanently over the forested mountains of the interior, past the misty crater lake of Grand Etang, and down the far side. There wasn't a birch tree within a thousand miles, and no Mighty Sparrow either, but he *was* on the car radio with a hit called "Lying Excuses":

The fact is she had on a bikinee,
And was attacked by African bees,
And very bravely I covered she,
With me whole body. . . .

So, what to do? "Go to Grenville, maan," some fellows on the corner suggested. "Dey havin' a calypso tent tonight." I took their advice: no matter what Grenadians called out at me from afar, I found them unfailingly helpful and friendly when approached. These "tents" are local calypso bands who compete for a place in Grenada's carnival, held early in August. Aspiring "calypsonians"—singer-composers—join a tent and show off their talents at public previews; those who get the best response are chosen to sing at carnival. It's a demanding art form, combining social comment, outrageous costume, risqué lyrics, musical *élan*, and sporting instinct. Grenadian "tents" are nowadays held indoors, this one in Grenville's vaguely art deco Cinema Deluxe. I got there early and bought a ticket with hours to spare.

To pass the time I went out to Pearls airport, the old landing strip superseded by Point Salines. What attracted me was a mark on the map indicating Carib remains, perhaps some interesting petroglyphs. But the relics I found were more recent. Here the invasion had surprised a Russian and a Cuban plane: hard evidence of the communist build-up threatening America's backyard. The Cyrillic lettering was unmistakable—CCCP—even though the canvas of the wings and fuselage was torn to ribbons and cows were chewing on it absent-mindedly. Canvas? Yes, this spearhead of the Eastern bloc was a biplane with a radial engine, obsolete long before the Cold War began. The Cuban presence was a little more impressive—a twin-engined turbo-prop airliner, circa 1960. It had been stuck here for repairs. The Americans thoroughly trashed them both, just to make sure.

The show was to start at 8:30, but by seven o'clock the streets around the cinema were boiling. It was almost dark and the cicadas had begun their own calypso—a syncopated screeching, interrupted by an insect that sounds exactly like an ambulance siren. The air was full of frangipani and cheap perfume. Cars and trucks were converging on the area, battling for right of way with horns and shouts. Knots of people went by, sucking on beer bottles, bobbing to ghetto-blasters on their shoulders. A man sailed through it all on an unlit motorbike, a flashlight in his mouth.

Eight-fifteen and the doors had not yet opened. The crowd, sensing that there mightn't be enough seats for all, had begun swarming at the entrance. A sea of hats and hair: natty dreads, afros, bald heads, shaven heads, women in cornrows and pirate scarves. There were tuques as big as pillowcases stuffed with Rastafarian locks, trilbies and pork pies, leather berets and Foreign Legion kepis. The entrance was protected by gates of welded reinforcing rod as massive as a gorilla cage. Men were climbing up the bars on the outside; people on the inside (how had they got in?) were throwing tickets out through the bars to their friends. At exactly half past eight a small door in the cage was parsimoniously opened by an enormous doorman. The crowd surged forward. My feet left the ground; I was suspended in a solid press of flesh. Someone called out, "White boy!" and offered instructions. I was swept under the bouncer's arm and into the auditorium. There must have been other entrances somewhere, because every seat, aisle, balcony, and ledge was already filled.

The nine-piece house band wore three red, three yellow, and three turquoise outfits—presumably intended to match the Grenadian flag. But they looked dowdy beside the calypsonians. There was Darius, dressed like a mediaeval jester with beatnik sunshades and a yellow beret; Shorty had an Indonesian print covered in sequins; Prince Joseph looked like a Pachuco gang-fighter; and Professor Shaggy had more glitter and more hair than Louis XIV. Their clothes flashed and winked and bounced off Singin' Emcee, who favoured a white silk zoot suit. They all took turns at the first number in honour of Carib Beer, sponsors of Kalypso Kastle, the name of Grenville's tent. I caught a line: *Whenever I'm in de bathroom I have a Carib in my hand....* The crowd clapped and yelled, and sang along. It was quite impossible to hear the rest. I felt like a swimmer in a millrace, at times submerged, at times borne aloft, as warm bodies and cold beer bottles squeezed and pushed and jumped. Those who had seats were standing on them; entire ranks of chairs began to rock. Hands shot out and grabbed hair for stability. Some Rastas started a discussion. Darius was singing something about apartheid: *Even Ronald Reagan supportin' South Africa!* Derisive applause broke out like a tropical storm. I came up for air and looked around—I was the only white marble in the place.

The midnight drive back to my hotel was long and interesting. Land crabs waved their claws and ran at the car like suicidal gladiators; dogs staged sit-down protests in the road. Even the cats gave me a hard stare before they strolled into the grass. The night creatures seemed to share the personality of this cocky, stubborn little island, one of the smallest sovereign nations in the world. But no matter how bold or quixotic Grenada surely is, I couldn't help thinking that awarding himself 8,612 medals for conquering it was a trifle self-indulgent of Uncle Sam.

TWELVE

Beyond Words

Most of the pieces gathered here were my own ideas, but sometimes an editor has given me a fortunate push in a new direction. I'd written for years about Latin America but never about the country where I lived. I'd explored the indigenous cultures of the Andes and Mesoamerica but not those of Canada.

Ever since my student days in Calgary, I'd been aware of the native people from the corner of my eye. There, on any downtown street, you saw Indian casualties from the winning of the west—drinkers, hookers, beggars—their tall frames stooped, their copper faces ruddy and swollen with alcohol. Most white Canadians hardly noticed them. They were simply "drunken Indians" unable to make their peace with "progress"—at best invisible, at worst an embarrassment. During Calgary's Stampede week, when prairie Indians put aside their cowboy clothes to bring out the ancient symbols of their culture, they received a kind of patronizing recognition. But once the dances were over and the tipis taken down, it was business as usual in the city's windy canyons.

Unpleasant facts occasionally showed up on the inside pages of the newspaper: a shoot-out on a Blackfoot reserve; a well-founded Indian land claim undercut by retroactive legislation; a United Nations report revealing that Canadian native people under twenty-five have the highest suicide rate of any population group on earth. I'd criticized Latin republics such as Peru and Guatemala for their repression of indigenous societies. But here, strewn across one of the world's wealthiest and supposedly most liberal countries, was social wreckage of an extremity I'd seldom seen in the Third World.

In 1988, *Saturday Night*'s senior editor, Barbara Moon—a husky-voiced smoker who had herself written eloquently on native issues—asked me to report on the struggle to save the Yukon's languages.

AFTER THE DESTRUCTION of the buffalo and the people who depended on them, a Canadian version of Tom Brown's schooldays was visited on the children of the survivors. In the archives you can see the photographs: Blackfoot boys in Eton jackets and leather boots, girls dressed like Victorian aunts, sad Asiatic faces staring bewildered and frightened from a private nightmare. The Indians were told that residential schools were for their own good: they had to be converted from pagans into Christians, from Stone Age hunters to Canadian citizens. Sometimes the schools were run by the federal government; often missionary groups were paid to do the job.

In the Yukon the boarding schools came more recently, and the experience is remembered bitterly by people, now in middle age, who were snatched from family and village to be incarcerated for ten, sometimes twelve months of the year during the formative stage of their lives. The aim was to break the continuity with one way of life and then imprint another. The teachers knew little about the subtleties of culture, but they understood that language was the key. If the language could be broken, then the culture—expressed and transmitted by language—could be killed.

Margaret Workman spent most of her early years in Aishihik, a small settlement about a hundred miles northwest of Whitehorse. There was no road or airstrip until she was about four, when white men began pouring into the Yukon, in the greatest numbers since the gold rush, to build the Alaska Highway during the Second World War. Her parents and grandparents spoke Southern Tutchone, a member of the great Athapaskan language family that includes Navajo and Apache as well as most Indian languages in the Yukon, Northwest Territories, and Alaskan interior. In the mid-1940s, at the age of seven, she was taken away to the Baptist Mission School in Whitehorse. She did not see her home again for nearly two years. Also at the school was her elder brother, but they were deliberately kept apart. Speaking their own language was punished with a beating.

"We were told to learn English, *instantly* like. And if they heard you saying anything in Indian you got the strap. Every chance we'd get, my brother and I, we used to sneak in behind the woodpile so we could speak in our language. I was one of them that got punished a lot." She smiles, but it's a rueful smile, a brave adult face on the child's pain. She's wearing an olive-green sweater and horn-rimmed glasses, and her black hair is neatly curled.

"To us it was a shocking thing," she continues. "I mean the cruelty of those Baptists, supposed to be Christian people, claiming to show us the right way of life. If they heard you speaking Indian they said it was the devil talking through you. We didn't know about religions. Religion to us was the way we lived, the land, the animals. We knew there was a creator, a god. But we'd never heard of Baptists and Anglicans, Protestants and Catholics. I don't think I learned too much in that school. It was morning prayers, evening prayers, Bible study. I only got to grade eight. My brother only made it to grade three. He kept running away. He couldn't take it."

I ask if she is still angry. She draws a breath, controlling a tremble that has crept into her voice.

"It took me quite a few years to forget. I've gotten over it a bit. But when I had my own children I never encouraged them with that kind of religion. I didn't want anything to do with it."

After her second year the missionaries took Margaret and other Aishihik children home for the summer, but indoctrination did not stop.

"A teacher came with us and set up a summer Bible school. We had lessons every day, so we couldn't leave the village. And because of that, Mum and Dad couldn't leave either. Normally they would go on their summer circuit, hunting caribou and moose, putting up dry meat and dry fish for the winter. And we would go with them to learn. But now they couldn't go because we had to attend Bible school."

"What we're talking about here," I venture, "is a concerted effort to destroy a culture."

Workman is direct: "It was cultural genocide to my way of thinking."

We are sitting in a classroom of the Whitehorse Elementary School, a classroom now devoted to lessons in Southern Tutchone and other Yukon languages. It's a square, bare institutional building: flat roof, cream stucco with blue trim; long passages and yellow rooms. But times and attitudes have changed. The old boarding schools have been closed. Now, through the Yukon Native Language Centre, at present based here, Margaret Workman and others like her are trying to bring back the languages that were beaten out of them a generation ago.

Seven Indian languages are spoken in the Yukon; six of them—Loucheux, Han, Northern Tutchone, Southern Tutchone, Kaska, and Tagish—are members of the Athapaskan family. As a rough analogy, these six are about as closely related to each other (and to the Dene languages of the Northwest Territories) as members of the Romance family. The seventh, Tlingit, is either a more distant relative or an "isolate"—a language on its own, like Basque.

Not every native Yukoner learned English through the schools. Gertie Tom, a few years older than Workman, was immersed in the outside world because of tuberculosis. During her twenties she spent three and a half years in an Edmonton isolation hospital. English lessons were one of the few activities that dispelled the boredom of her long convalescence.

After she returned to Whitehorse in 1961 she worked as a bilingual radio announcer with the CBC. In 1977 two people came to see her: John Ritter, a linguist, and Julie Cruikshank, an anthropologist. They asked her to help them develop a programme to document and teach native languages.

"Before that I hadn't thought much about my language—being in hospital so long, speaking English, I'd begun to forget. When John and Julie started asking me questions, I realized I was losing it. But now, after working here, I'm thinking Indian again!"

With Ritter and Cruikshank, she devised a spelling system for Northern Tutchone. As the Yukon Native Language Centre expanded, with Ritter as director, she began developing materials for the instructors who teach Northern Tutchone in Whitehorse and elsewhere. To the uninitiated, the spelling system looks complex. Athapaskan languages have many more phonemes—distinct sounds—than English, so our alphabet has to be expanded by a daunting array of diacritical marks and special consonants.

I ask for a beginner's lesson.

Dắninch'i?	How are you?
Sáw!	Fine!
Yi ech'õ dajän?	What is this?
Dajan dí ech'i	This is tea.

The words come to life on her lips, a musical, nasal sound. Like many Athapaskan languages, Northern Tutchone is tonal; to a stranger's ear it sounds Oriental, almost Chinese. It differs from its closest relative, Southern Tutchone, by having many of the tones reversed—what is high in Northern will be low in Southern, and vice versa. For example, "his/her head" in Northern is *utthí*—the acute accent representing a rising pitch on the final vowel; in Southern, the word is almost the same, but the pitch falls at the end. Within each language, as in Chinese, tones may indicate different meanings for words that are otherwise identical: in Southern Tutchone, *ts'àl* is "spoon" but *ts'al* means "frog".

Gertie Tom has also been publishing stories and legends in bilingual editions. Her most recent book is *Èkeyi: Gyò Cho Chú, My Country: Big Salmon River*, a volume of autobiography, genealogy, folklore, and photography bringing alive the placenames of the country—a country "where the mountains are nameless" according to Robert W. Service. They are nameless only in English.

Some Tutchone toponyms are so ancient they defy translation. As with "London" or "Kent", their origins have been lost as the language has contracted and changed. Ts'ändlia Mãn, for example, has no clear translation. Mãn means "lake", but Ts'ändlia is simply a name, although Gertie Tom remembers an ancient story about that place:

> *There was no food and people were beginning to starve. Men hunted for moose without any success.... They didn't even get a grouse, not even a rabbit.... Then they started to dig holes through the ice.... Still they couldn't catch a thing. No matter how hard they tried, they couldn't get any fish.*
>
> *They couldn't even get a rabbit.... All of those people starved to death, they say. That's what the old people say happened around Ts'ändlia a long time ago.... There is no English name for that lake.*

Other placenames clearly summarize a story. Hudzì Cho Yę Ts'intsí ("He Cried about a Big Caribou") tells about a hunter who failed to shoot a giant reindeer. Tthę̨l Tadétth'ät ("Stone Axe Got Lost") recalls the loss of a Yukoner's most basic tool. Losing an axe was no mere annoyance; it was a disaster comparable, in our terms, to vehicle breakdown in the wilderness. No axe: no firewood, no tentpoles, no holes in the ice.

In this heated, sterile building, with a Keg restaurant on a nearby corner, the time of which these stories tell seems as remote as the age of Beowulf. My gaze strays out of the window to the smooth, dark mountains that surround Whitehorse like a pod of breaching whales. In those days, if you had no luck hunting or fishing, you starved; if you couldn't find firewood, you froze. The land was not the fragile, vanquished thing it is today, trampled by roads and railways, riddled by mines. It was omnipotent. The people had no towns, or even cabins. They lived in moss shelters and skin tents. They had to move to find their livelihood. Only their understanding of this land and its ways stood between life and death. That is the exacting culture enshrined in these names and words, a culture whose very survival for thousands of years proved its fitness in this place.

About fifty native languages are still spoken in Canada, almost all of them in serious trouble. The healthiest are found in the Northwest Territories, where native people still form the majority of the population; the weakest are those isolated on the archipelago of small reserves surrounded by a Euro-Canadian sea. Those of the Yukon fall somewhere in between. Approximately a third of the Yukon's 25,000 people are Indian or part-Indian, but outside Whitehorse, where half the territorial population lives, the native proportion is higher. The impact of boarding schools and other outside pressures has been devastating. Only about a third of Yukon Indians are fluent in a native language, and most of them are above the age of thirty. A wedge has been driven through the culture: people of Margaret Workman's generation are generally bilingual, able to communicate in "Indian" with their elders and in English with their children. But between grandparents and grandchildren yawns a gulf as wide as that between pre-Columbian Europe and America, and into it the knowledge, art, and history of centuries are tumbling to extinction.

Since 1977, the Yukon Native Language Centre has grown from a tiny operation in a basement office to an organization with a yearly budget of about half a million dollars. Native language teachers from all over the territory now come here for training. One morning I sit in on the grade-five class taught by Jane Montgomery and Polly Fraser. Montgomery is from Old Crow, a Loucheux community. (Her mother, Edith Josie, is well known in the Yukon as a radio broadcaster and journalist.) The class is in Southern Tutchone, which Montgomery can understand but does not speak perfectly. At this level it doesn't matter: Polly Fraser, who is fluent in Southern Tutchone, demonstrates the correct phrasing and pronunciation while learning classroom techniques from Montgomery.

It's many years since I was at school and this class is unlike anything I remember. The desks are pushed down at the far end of the room. There are no lists of gerunds on the blackboard, no inkwells and little vocabulary books, no bored and baffled kids.

"We're going to play a new game today called 'Shaking Hands'," Montgomery announces, telling the children to gather in pairs.

"If I say three sentences and it's all animals, you shake hands. If it's two people and one animal you have to change places."

There are ten girls and six boys. All but two or three are native. From their bright, attentive faces you can tell they enjoy this class. They listen to the teachers with heads cocked like birds, keen to be the first to recognize the sequence. Then there are scuffles and laughter as the set is broken and children change partners. For the white children, Southern Tutchone is obviously far more foreign than French or Latin; but most of the others will have a chance to practise what they're learning whenever they see their grandparents. They'll be able to surprise their elders with some phrases, and that may encourage the older people to use the language in front of the children instead of struggling along in broken English. In this way, perhaps, the wedge between the generations can be shaken loose.

After class, John Ritter takes me up to a hillside overlooking Whitehorse, where the low wood and concrete buildings of the new Yukon College are taking shape among spruce and pines. We stop at a trailer for a pair of hard hats.

"Every time I start feeling burned out I come up here," he says. The excursion is visibly a tonic. His pink, boyish face lights up with visions of what the Centre will be able to accomplish when it moves here next summer. The space is impressive—a soundproof studio for recording audio tapes, a library, classrooms, and a sunny reception area with a glass roof.

"One of the many great things about this place is that elders won't have to struggle up three flights of stairs any more."

It is hard to get Ritter to talk about himself. Eventually he reveals that he grew up in West Virginia and studied at Michigan State. After four years of graduate work in theoretical linguistics at MIT he went to Fort McPherson in the Northwest Territories to study Athapaskan. In the mid-seventies he moved to the Yukon. Two years later he started on Northern Tutchone with Gertie Tom in Whitehorse.

"In 1977, Daniel Tlen went to Ottawa and came back with some money to keep things going. We never dreamed then that we'd be where we are now. But what happened is that more and more people got interested. They started to come to us with old stories and songs, some of them in archaic dialect. 'I know this is my language,' they'd say, 'but even I don't understand what some of the words mean.' And we'd sit down and try to work it out. It's been rewarding beyond my fondest expectations."

The question many outsiders ask is, why? Why should we make such an effort to support languages spoken by only a few hundred people?

"For me," Ritter answers, "these languages—any languages—have intrinsic value and beauty. For the natives themselves the purpose is much more concrete. Even if they don't speak them much, the languages are as much a part of their identity as Latin or Chaucer is of ours. We may not speak Latin or archaic English, but we place a high value on knowing something about them. At the very least, Athapaskan languages can fulfil a ceremonial and cultural role. On the other hand, it is quite possible that several of them *will* come back. It has happened with Welsh and modern Hebrew. We're only beginning here. Already the kids have a lively interest in knowing their Indian names and genealogies. And we're working very hard on the placenames, which have a direct relevance to land claims.

"A major aspect is the matter of pride. Until this programme started, almost all the teachers in the Yukon were non-native. It's hard to overestimate how good the kids feel about seeing a native person in the school as a teacher instead of as a cleaner."

"I am always sorry when any language is lost," Dr. Johnson said more than two centuries ago, "because languages are the pedigree of nations." I believe he meant two things by that admirable sentence: first, that a language contains the experience, history, and expression of a people; second, that we should be concerned by the death of *any* language, because all, as John Ritter observes, have intrinsic value as human artifacts, as responses to experience.

Our age is an age of extinction. In the past fifty years the earth has lost more species of animals and plants than in the preceding two thousand. It is the same with languages and cultures. Global civilization has spread at the expense of others. The death of a language is the equivalent of a species dying out. Diversity is being replaced by what farmers call monoculture—reliance on a single crop—just as prairie flowers and grasses have been swept away by acres of wheat. Monoculture may be more efficient in the short run, but long-term adaptability and strength depend on diversity. We should never forget that the Irish potato famine occurred because all the tubers of Ireland were descended from the same plant, and therefore fatally vulnerable to a single disease.

A language is not simply a medium of communication. It is a description of the world; it shapes and is shaped by culture and environment; it imposes categories on inchoate experience; it orders and articulates those categories in a way that is unique. The precise view of the world in one language may not be communicable in another, and the aesthetic quality of that vision often defies the most skilful interpreter. We are all familiar with slight differences in categorization between European languages. We will say the French or the Germans "have a word for it" and we'll use *chic* or *Weltschmerz* for some quality that English has not elaborated. When one compares languages that have nothing historically in common, major incompatibilities of cognition may appear. In English we cannot speak about a person (except in the plural) without specifying his or her sex. In French, and most other European languages, even the inanimate world is arbitrarily divided up into male and female. Speakers of Athapaskan, which has no gender, must be baffled by our fascination with it. Can it be that a sex-conscious language expresses, influences, and reinforces a sex-conscious culture? (After all, "macho" is a Spanish word.) Could Arab culture function as it does without its strongly gender-marked language? But are Hungarians less sexist than Austrians because their language has no gender and German does? This is tricky ground and there are no simple answers. The relationship between language, thought, and culture is so intimate that no one has successfully unravelled it. While lack of superfluous gender may not necessarily imply egalitarian treatment of the sexes in real life, the converse has certainly become regarded as implicit sexism by English-speaking feminists. We now have moves to replace "mankind" with "humankind", even to search for a single pronoun instead of he/she/it. Other cultural values are much more subtly and deeply entrenched. Consider the semantic relationship of "human" and "humane". And what might the resonance between "God", "good", and "goods" say about our attitude to property?

Until fifteen or twenty years ago, Canada's native languages were ignored when they were not attacked. In 1967, the report of the Royal Commission on Bilingualism and Biculturalism mentioned them only in passing, to say that they lay outside the scope of an inquiry restricted to Canada's two "founding" peoples. Canada exposed itself by those words as a white-settler state without room for those who have lived here since long before Cabot and Cartier. To that mentality, native languages were mere casualties of progress: primitive, simple, incapable of adapting to the modern world.

A few had known better. Emile Petitot, a French Catholic priest and linguist active in the Yukon a century ago, was astonished to find Athapaskan languages more complex morphologically and phonetically than his own. He did not shrink from making an invidious comparison:

> *We have, in effect, before our eyes this flagrant contradiction: on the one hand, logical—I would even say philosophical—languages, rich in varied terms... the expression of a high intelligence; and on the other, ignorant remnants of peoples, incapable of lofty ideas.... It is like seeing the perfect image of a beautiful man, dead or dying.*

He was writing before the Klondike gold rush, and the decline he saw—the initial effect of foreign traders and diseases—was nothing compared to what would shortly follow. The story of the Klondike needs no repeating here. It is enough to recall that within two years the village of Dawson grew from a small trading and fishing camp to the largest city west of Winnipeg and north of San Francisco. By the end of 1898 it held 30,000 people—more than the entire population of the Yukon today.

As you drive north from Whitehorse to Dawson through some of the most ascetic grandeur on the continent, it is easy to be seduced by Service's vision of an empty land "waiting for man to come". The tree line is low. Bald mountains and expanses of tundra rise above the forests, gilded with weak sunshine, dusted with drifts of snow. The rivers, too, are deserted. The sternwheelers that once plied them have been broken up for scrap or pulled ashore as tourist attractions. The canoes and moose-skin boats of the Indians have vanished. At long intervals you come to a tiny settlement: a scattering of cabins, a few trailers, some heavy machinery, a ramshackle restaurant offering dubious hamburgers and spartan rooms. But this desertion is recent. The Indians who once roamed hundreds of miles following moose, caribou, and traplines were resettled by government decree around white towns during the 1950s, with effects as devastating as those of the boarding schools. Boredom prompted alcoholism and family strife. Cramped living in plywood shacks aided the spread of tuberculosis. If the Yukon looks empty now, it is because the roads and the federal government swept the people from the land.

Not far from Dawson, you come upon a place that seems to have been the scene of a terrible convulsion. It goes on for miles: great rifts and trenches; pools of black, stagnant water; rippling ridges of gravel like the casts of giant worms. Nothing lives in the ponds, nothing grows on the piles of tailings. The land has been stripped, sifted, and abandoned. This was not, of course, the work of woolly sourdoughs with picks and shovels. This was done by steam dredgers that came after the little men went home.

Left with this mess were the people who had been here long before the gold rush: the Han Indians. Archaeological excavations at the Han village of Moosehide (two miles north of Dawson and accessible only by boat or footpath) revealed that people have been camping here for more than 6,000 years. The village gets its name from the scar of an old landslide on the hill above it. The story of the name was told years ago by Mary McLeod. Ironically, it is about the transformation of the world by technology, but here the outcome was positive. A stone axe enabled the Indians to vanquish a mythical race of man-eaters:

> *In early days there were cannibals everywhere and they bothered people. So one time people climb hill near where is now Moosehide to get above them. Lots of big trees on these hills that time. People had only axe made of sharp rock in those days. They cut down the biggest tree with stone axe and they throw that tree down the hill on cannibals. That tree start big slide. It kill all the cannibals. That slide is shaped like hide of moose so people call that place Moosehide.*

Before the first gold strike on their lands in 1886, the Han probably numbered about a thousand, scattered in small groups. In the next fifteen years they passed from the Stone Age to the steam age, from shamanism to Christianity, from nomadic hunting to a cash economy. Some worked as labourers, others supplied Dawson City and the camps with wood and meat. A few Indians became rich but, with the abrupt collapse of the boom, most of them were left with nothing. Their own way of life had been changed irrevocably, and the new way they had so rapidly embraced suddenly packed up and left.

The diseases the whites had brought did not depart so readily. In 1907, several hundred Han were living at Moosehide; by 1932, after waves of smallpox, influenza, typhus, and mumps, only fifty-six remained. Some had moved to the clapboard ruins of Dawson, but there's no doubt that the population suffered a massive decline. Mediaeval Europe's culture was seriously disrupted by the loss of a third of its population during the Black Death. In the Dawson area, as elsewhere in the Americas, the demographic collapse following contact with outsiders was between 70 and 90 per cent.

Ancient Han culture passed into oblivion before much of it could be recorded. It was presumably similar to that of the more numerous Loucheux, who live further north in the Old Crow area and speak a closely related language. Pre-contact Athapaskan society was not rigidly structured. There were no permanent settlements or political institutions, no organized religion. The world had been created by a Trickster hero, often identified with the Crow or Raven, who was full of wisdom, pranks, and zen-like paradoxes. The dead were reincarnated as humans and occasionally as animals. Curing and divining were carried out by shamans in contact with spirit-helpers (often animals) and other powers. Individuals also had their own spirit-helpers, usually acquired during adolescence, when girls were secluded and boys underwent arduous training. As influence spread into the Yukon from the elaborate societies of the Northwest Coast, concepts of rank, wealth, lineage, and potlatching were adopted. This trend accelerated rapidly during the heyday of the fur trade in the last century, but the system was later eroded by missionary pressure, intermarriage with whites, and epidemics.

Since the 1930s the Han population has begun to recover. By the mid-1960s there were some 250 in the Dawson area; today there are 400—approximately one-third of Dawson residents. But the language has not made a corresponding comeback.

"Our Han language is almost no more," Chief Angie Joseph tells me when I attend a band council meeting at the attractive Chief Isaac Memorial Centre. "Don't ask us to say anything—we'd have to go home and look it up in our books!" She explains that the Yukon Native Language Centre organized a short language course in Dawson last spring, taught by Archie Roberts, one of fewer than a dozen fluent Han speakers left in the Yukon.

"We're almost a dying race—let's put it that way," Joseph adds with a laugh. It's a bitter joke, uncomfortably close to the truth. The band councillors are in their twenties and thirties, members of a generation that grew up speaking only English. The final break came in 1957, when the federal government suspended services to the old log village at Moosehide and made its inhabitants move to Dawson City. Archie Roberts remembers how things changed after his childhood years in the 1930s:

"Everyone spoke Han in the village in them days. We used to have our own Indian constable and Indian court. But after we moved into Dawson all that stopped. You heard less and less of the language as the elders died off."

I ask who besides himself is left—how many people can have a conversation in Han? He has to think hard, slowly counting off eight or nine friends and relatives on his fingers. "Then there's some in Eagle, Alaska, that know it," he adds. Even including those, the total is small—about thirty-five fluent Han speakers in the whole world. He's a softspoken, amiable man with a winning smile. He seems reticent. I try to imagine the loneliness, the sense of loss. To be fully at home only in a dying language is comparable to... what? Creeping amnesia? No, amnesia isn't the right analogy: the memories are all there, the stories and legends, the personal and public history. It is the ability to share those things that is fading. His situation is like that of a person gradually losing the power of speech itself. The past is a great mansion reduced to a few inhabited rooms. Before long the number of occupants will dwindle to three, to two; and then the last person left will become locked in an isolation from which there can be no release but death. No matter how much English that person may acquire as a substitute, he or she will be alone with everything in Han language and culture that is untranslatable: rhetoric, poetry, aesthetics, and ways of apprehending a world for which English has no words or thoughts.

In Carcross, an hour's drive south of Whitehorse, a memorial potlatch is being held for Angela Sidney's daughter, who died a year ago. I am with Jeff Leer, a linguist from the University of Alaska at Fairbanks, who has worked with Angela Sidney and other elders for several years. When we arrive, the sun is low above the black spruce forests and whaleback mountains that rise behind the settlement. An old clapboard hotel and a sternwheeler pulled up on dry land beside the railway tracks are already in evening shadow. About two hundred people have gathered in the Tagish band hall for a banquet, to be followed by speeches and a ceremonial handing out of gifts. In the old days cremation was the Tagish custom; memorial potlatches were held when the ashes of the deceased were placed in a mortuary house about a year after the funeral. Nowadays the Tagish are mostly Anglicans, and potlatches celebrate instead the raising of a gravestone.

We are late; the meal of moosemeat and fish is ending, bowls of fruit salad are being passed around. Leer introduces me to Mrs. Sidney. She is eighty-five years old and the last fluent speaker of the Tagish language. She takes our hands and holds them as if we were long-lost relatives. Fine white hair falls over her shoulders like a waterfall captured on slow film; her black eyes twinkle with warmth and intelligence. Around her neck is a wooden carving of a mythological beaver, her clan crest. She also wears a ceremonial gold and purple headband and, like many others present, a jacket emblazoned with a large black crow, the emblem of her moiety or societal half. The moiety system divides society into two equal and complementary "teams". Crows always marry Wolves, and vice versa. The hosting of potlatches is divided in the same way. This is a Crow event—Wolves are invited, but only Crows contribute to the expenses and hand out gifts.

One of Angela Sidney's creation stories tells how the division was ordained by Crow when he made people, after creating the land and sea:

> *After that he walks around, flies around all alone. He's tired. He's lonely. He needs people. He took poplar tree bark.... He carved it. Then he breathed into it.*
>
> *"Live," he said. And he made person. He made Crow and Wolf too. At first they can't talk to each other. Crow man and woman are shy with each other—look away. Wolf people same way.*
>
> *"This is no good," he said. So he changed that. He made Crow man sit with Wolf woman and he made Wolf man sit with Crow woman. So Crow must marry Wolf and Wolf must marry Crow.*
>
> *That's how the world began.*

Angela Sidney is also a member of the Order of Canada, an honour she received in 1986 for a lifetime of community health work and her efforts to help specialists document the Tagish language. While there is hope that other Yukon languages may be saved from extinction, Tagish has reached the point of no return. All that can be done now is to compile an archive. Mrs Sidney's situation is not quite the same as that of Archie Roberts. She herself is Tlingit on her mother's side, so while that language survives, the death of Tagish is only a partial occlusion of the past. When she tells stories, she often mixes the two languages, reflecting how Tagish was ousted not by English but by Tlingit. Before the gold rush broke their power, the Tlingit people, who extend through southeastern Alaska and northwestern British Columbia, controlled the Yukon passes and dominated trade between coast and interior. The Tagish, always a small group, came under heavy Tlingit influence, intermarrying, adopting customs, and finally abandoning Tagish for the Tlingit language. Ironically, Tlingit itself is now endangered. Angela Sidney has done what she can: she has poured all she remembers of Tagish into tapes, books, and archives. It has been her life's work. Perhaps it is not too late for Tlingit, the language of her mother's people. "Now it's up to the young people to spend time with the elders," she tells us. Then she takes Jeff Leer's hand: "And to friends like you. You must teach the Indian language." When the meal is finished, she makes a speech in Tlingit. When she has finished, some young people pick up drums and sing the words of a ritual song:

Du yaa kanagúdi
Shéiyadi Yéil
Ash yát kanalgwatlch yáx̱
Du yaa nagúdi
Du G̱oojí yinaadé.

(The Crow's strut
His walk
Is like he's swaggering
Showing off
Before the Wolf.)

The MC, an imposing figure in a well-filled red jacket, microphone in hand, then calls the Crows to line up and contribute to the potlatch fund. After each donation he sings out the name of the giver and the amount. The otherness of Tagish culture suddenly comes to me. We would shrink from such behaviour, but the essence of a potlatch is reciprocal display. The size of the gift carries many messages besides generosity. It announces, for example, the closeness of one's kin ties to the host, the degree of obligation incurred at past potlatches thrown by the opposite moiety, and the standing of the giver in the community. All is carefully noted in a book, and in the long run, I'm told, accounts keep remarkably even. Even though most people are speaking English, and the gifts distributed are mainly things like socks, sweaters, and windshield scrapers, the structure and essence of the ancient potlatch endure.

In the dining room of the only hotel in Ross River, a sign says: SAME SHIT, DIFFERENT DAY. White men in gimme caps and muddy workboots are feeding on piles of chips and huge wedges of pie. There's a smell of wet plaid, stewed coffee, and stale cigarettes. The wall by the telephone is covered in scrawled messages. Business is booming. A new gold mine is opening up. No one is quite sure how it will affect the local Indians, who have so far avoided many of the problems suffered by the Han. Ross River is in the eastern Yukon beyond the Big Salmon mountains, and three-quarters of the four hundred people here are native. Many still hunt and trap, and they fear that game animals will be scared off if there is too much prospecting. A land claim settlement is urgent. Forested hills rise behind frame houses, a gas station, and one or two Quonset huts. A couple of blocks away the scattered log cabins of the Indians begin, and between the two is a new cedar building containing a native-owned co-op store and offices of the Kaska-Dena band.

Kaska, the main language here apart from English, is spoken fluently by about a third of the Indian population and understood to some extent by another third. Several families also speak the Slavey language of Fort Norman, Northwest Territories, which has had links with Ross River for hundreds, perhaps thousands, of years.

"We are all part of the Athapaskan people," Chief Hammond Dick tells me at the band office. "We've had this relationship with Fort Norman for a long time—long before that border was set up." He waves his hand in the direction of the territorial boundary, about 130 miles to the east. "We used to trade, marry—and fight battles with each other."

On the wall of his small office I notice a Chinese zodiac.

"I'm interested in that," he says. "I like to remind myself that the white culture isn't the only one out there. I'm impressed how the Chinese people in Canada manage to keep their culture going."

He's a vigorous, handsome man in his late thirties, his ease in English the legacy of boarding school.

"Until I was seven I used to travel on the land with my parents, speaking Indian. Then the church and the government said that withholding children from school was against the law. So I and other kids my age, we were pulled from the community and taken away. I was one of the last to go through that Baptist mission school in Whitehorse before it was closed down. There was fear there. They punished us for speaking our language. Now we're trying to bring it back."

He explains how the elders have given direction, emphasizing the importance of Kaska not only in language courses but in official and ceremonial contexts. "During our annual General Assembly we translated everything to the elders and to the public. It was tedious but people realized the importance. When you've been brought up to be ashamed of speaking your own language, it helps to see it given respect that way."

The Ross River school is a dark cedar building, only a few years old but already sinking into the permafrost, a reminder that white technology has not been able to dominate everything in the north. Inside, it has a bright, welcoming atmosphere. Small children huddle around their teachers on the carpeted floors. The walls are covered in cut-outs—animals, calendars, colourful games.

Patrick Moore, the linguist who developed the language programme here, is at his Macintosh computer in the library, typing in a Kaska font he invented. He's a slight, blond man of thirty-three, studious, quietly assertive. He introduces me to the native teachers, Josephine Acklack and Grady Sterriah.

Besides teaching, Acklack and Sterriah help Moore to document placenames and local histories. They are also compiling a dictionary of Kaska, an endless task, as any lexicographer knows. All these languages have rich vocabularies for hunting, trapping, and describing topography. There are elaborate ways of defining the movements of water and wind, the varying quality of vegetation, seasonal habits of wildlife, the shape, sound, and smell of the land. Direction is indicated not by the cardinal points but by the flow of rivers—a system that makes sense in a land where the sun almost disappears each winter. A single word can express place and direction as precisely as a whole sentence in English. *Yeenàn-jìt*, for example, breaks down as follows: *yee* = "quite a way", *nàn* = "across [a river or lake] from where we are standing", *jì* = "downstream", and the final *t* indicates the point intended. The phrase is much more precise than translation makes it seem. Early geographers in the Yukon were astonished how easily Indians who had never seen pencil or paper in their lives could sit down and draw detailed, accurate maps.

"People here still use the land a lot," Moore emphasizes. "There are some who live out there all year round. So our language programme isn't just classroom work. The kids go out on the land with elders whenever possible. In that way they experience the language at work."

On Tuesdays Ross River has its culture night. In 1983, the band council came up with the idea of renewing historical ties with Fort Norman as a way of reviving traditional culture. In the old days, the Fort Norman people would camp at Ross River on their trading and trapping expeditions. Drumming and "stick gambling" went on all night by the light of huge bonfires. Quantities of furs, tobacco, and tea were lost and won. Those days are gone, but for the past four years the Fort Norman drummers have been coming back to Ross River to teach the old songs and gambling games. Every week as many as fifty people gather at the band hall to practise what they have learned. In the stick game (or hand game) two rows of players face each other cross-legged on the ground. One team conceals a number of small objects in fists and folded arms; their oppponents have to guess where the objects are hidden. It is similar to chess players deciding who goes first, but much more lively and complex. There is a great show of bobbing and hiding, and triumphant shouts at every inspired guess. With the game goes a fast, hard beat and wild, whooping songs.

Anyone who has never experienced Dene drums at close quarters will be unprepared. They are large, shallow tambourines, with caribou membranes kept tight by heating over a fire or stove. The sound they produce is metallic and very loud. Half a dozen such drums can dominate a hall filled with hundreds of dancers. Each drummer attacks his instrument with tremendous energy, singing at the top of his voice to force the words through the barrage of sound. If you resist the beat it will drive you from the room. If you accept it, let it penetrate, it fills you with an extraordinary sensation of immediacy and power. The drums become the centre of the world.

Whitehorse, population 15,000, seems large and cosmopolitan after a week on the road. I feel I have no answers. I still do not know if these languages will be here in thirty or forty years. But it is clear that the future demands more of native people than of whites. If their cultures are to survive, the Yukon Indians must live in two worlds, not just one.

A nation, it has been said, is only as great as the way it treats its minorities. How Canada has prospered at the expense of the lands and lives of its indigenous people is the country's greatest shame.

In one of Angela Sidney's stories, two old women live in the underworld:

> *One is supposed to be sleeping; the other holds up the earth, with a pole. When she shakes it, that's when there is supposed to be an earthquake. That old lady there with the pole is...death. She always argues. She's the one who always says:*
>
> *"Let people sleep for good when they go to sleep. Let them die."*
>
> *That Death Woman always wants to kill people before their time.*

But Sleep Woman allows people to rest, and renews the gift of life when they awake. For the past hundred years, Death Woman has had the upper hand with the native people of the Yukon. Their world has been shaken by catastrophe: invasion, disease, rapid and destructive change. Perhaps now that period is ending. Perhaps they, and we white intruders, can wake from the grasp of Death Woman, and see that two futures are possible: a native future as well as a Canadian one.

THIRTEEN

Does Canada Want a Wounded Knee?

After the Yukon trip I followed the native situation in Canada more closely. Between 1987 and 1990, the federal government tried to amend the Canadian constitution with the Meech Lake Accord. This involved transferring federal powers to the provinces in order to persuade the mainly French province of Quebec that it would have little to gain by carrying out its frequent threat to secede. The accord became highly unpopular outside Quebec. Above all, it alarmed indigenous people—Indians, Métis, and Inuit—because it threatened to undermine their rights. Canada's first inhabitants were shunted aside in the negotiations and outraged by the politicians' view of Canada as a product of two "founding peoples", both white.

By a fluke (due to shortage of time), Manitoba's legislature required a unanimous vote to introduce the accord for ratification. One member of that legislature was an Indian, the first ever to sit there. In June 1990, Elijah Harper, a Cree, killed the hated accord with a shake of his head and an eagle feather in his hand.

That was only the beginning of what became known as Canada's Indian summer. The Quebec town of Oka, near

Montreal, had been trying for years to expand a golf course on land claimed by the neighbouring Kanehsatake Mohawks—merely the latest move in a 300-year history of white encroachment. Things came to a head when the Mohawks put up barricades and the mayor of Oka ordered a police assault. In a brief, chaotic gunfight on July 11, one policeman died. The Indians held their ground and were soon supported by fellow Mohawks at the much larger territory of Kahnawake, just across the St. Lawrence River from downtown Montreal. These Mohawks closed city highways and the Mercier Bridge crossing their land. Both Indian territories were promptly encircled and besieged, at first by police, later by thousands of Canadian troops.

Despite the gravity of the crisis, Prime Minister Brian Mulroney refused to recall Canada's parliament from summer recess. Without Parliament, no state of emergency could be declared; without such a declaration, normal civil liberties could not legally be suspended or infringed. Yet the federal and Quebec governments blithely trampled the rights of many people—especially Indians, journalists, and negotiators—and in so doing violated Canada's constitution.

At this time I had just completed a draft of my fourth book, *Stolen Continents*, a history of the Americas from Columbus to the present emphasizing Indian sources so as to see the other side of the familiar saga. I concentrated on five peoples: Aztec, Maya, Inca, Cherokee, and Iroquois. Mohawks are Iroquois, one of six member nations in the Iroquois Confederacy, an ancient polity recognized in numerous treaties with Britain and other European powers. The Confederacy has never surrendered its independence to Canada, either by treaty or by conquest. The fundamental issues—still ignored by Canada—that underlay the 1990 Mohawk crisis were sovereignty and jurisdiction.

Having just researched Iroquois history, I was in a position to evaluate statements coming from Prime Minister Mulroney, Premier Bourassa of Quebec, and other sources. I was appalled by what I heard. Were the governments of Canada and Quebec really so ignorant of their own past relations with these Indians? Or were they lying to their citizens and to the world in the hope that nobody would know any better?

"Does Canada Want a Wounded Knee?" was published by *The Globe and Mail* on August 30, 1990, in the final weeks of the Mohawk siege.

SINCE ROBERT BOURASSA, Premier of Quebec, ordered the Canadian army to move against the Mohawks of Kanehsatake and Kahnawake near Montreal, he has tried to justify his action by saying he has to defend democracy against people who do not believe in it. Perhaps he has forgotten that Indians were not allowed to vote in his province until 1968.

Perhaps he has forgotten that many Mohawks' first experience of Canada's democracy was when the Mounties overthrew their traditional chiefs at gunpoint. Not just once, not in the remote past, but several times within the past hundred years. During one of these putsches, at Akwesasne in 1899, Canadian police shot dead an unarmed Mohawk chief.

The Iroquois Confederacy, also called the League of Six Nations, is in fact the oldest democracy on this continent. Its political system, which includes a voice for all and a balance of power between the sexes, existed when Europe still believed in the divine right of kings. Many know, even if Mr. Bourassa does not, that this ancient federation inspired Benjamin Franklin and other fathers of the United States. The eagle on the American shield is an Iroquois eagle, and the arrows in its grasp originally were not thirteen but six—representing the Mohawk, Oneida, Onondaga, Cayuga, Seneca, and Tuscarora, who lived from the St. Lawrence to the Ohio.

Mr. Bourassa likes to ask the press—especially the European press—what they would do if a part of Paris, for example, armed itself and blockaded roads. His analogy is false. Unlike New France, the Mohawk Nation has never been conquered—not by Britain, nor by Canada; certainly not by Quebec. On the contrary, for more than two centuries the Iroquois Confederacy held the balance of power in North America. Without Iroquois help the British might never have defeated the French, or kept Canada from the Americans. Perhaps this bothers Mr. Bourassa.

Prime Minister Mulroney, who seems these days to take his cue from Mr. Bourassa, dismisses Mohawk claims to sovereignty as "bizarre". When he managed to tear himself away from the aura of weightier matters surrounding President Bush, he said that the Mohawks were seeking to "give themselves" the status of an independent nation. He held this up as an example of how absurd their demands had become. He, too, must have forgotten that the Iroquois not only are unconquered but have never surrendered their sovereignty to anyone. They possess treaties stating clearly that they and Britain are equal partners in a military and political alliance. They ask only that these treaties be respected by Britain's successor, Canada.

This is not, as Mulroney and Bourassa might have us believe, a quaint historical curiosity kept alive by cranks and radicals. It is an issue that the Confederacy has raised consistently in modern times. The Iroquois have taken it to Ottawa, to London, and, when they were blocked in both those places, to Geneva, travelling on their own passports in the 1920s. Their sovereignty claim was sufficiently strong that the League of Nations was prepared to hear it in 1923. Britain, having told the Iroquois it could do nothing because the matter lay within Canada's jurisdiction, was nevertheless willing to threaten the Six Nations' friends—Holland, Persia, and others—with serious diplomatic consequences to get the matter dropped.

A few months later, the Canadian government moved to crush the last of the Confederacy governments. On October 7, 1924, armed Mounties burst into the Six Nations Council at Ohsweken (near Brantford, Ontario), read out a proclamation dissolving the ancient assembly, broke open the safe, and seized treaty documents, many of them germane to the sovereignty case. More police burst into homes and took away wampum belts—the Iroquois symbols of government, their equivalents of flag, mace, and Magna Carta.

Puppet "elected" councils were then set up under police direction. From that day until this, only a small fraction of Iroquois have accepted these councils as legitimate, yet they are the only ones recognized by Canadian law.

Soon after this, in a piece of legislation worthy of South Africa, the Canadian Indian Act of 1927 made it illegal for anyone to raise money for the purpose of taking Indian land and sovereignty claims to court. This racist and repressive law stayed in effect until the 1950s. Small wonder that the Mohawks do not trust what Kim Campbell, the federal Justice minister, calls "one of the finest legal systems in the world".

When the Confederacy chiefs tried to take back their Council House in 1959, they were again ousted by club-wielding Mounties. But they have not gone away. They are gaining in strength both in Canada and in the United States, and the more progressive of the "elected" chiefs have wisely begun to defer to their authority. Until the Canadian government acknowledges that it has treated the Iroquois the way the CIA treats banana republics, and until it allows them to restore their own political system, there will always be young men with guns ready to step into the breach.

Mr. Mulroney and Mr. Bourassa also talk as if the loss of Iroquois land is something that belongs to the remote past. In truth, many Mohawks have lost more land since 1930 than in the previous hundred years. They have lost it to compulsory purchase by white governments eager to build bridges such as the blockaded Mercier, hydroelectric dams, and the St. Lawrence Seaway cheaply at Indian expense. As a result, fishing—a major food source for these Mohawks—has been destroyed at Kahnawake; and at Akwesasne land and water have been polluted so severely by heavy industries attracted by cheap power that neither farming nor fishing is safe.

Small wonder that some Mohawks have turned to gambling, "smuggling", and other unsavoury ways to survive. Of course, it is only smuggling if one denies Mohawk sovereignty. Whites, not Indians, drew the Canada/U.S. border through the middle of Akwesasne.

Mr. Mulroney has claimed that Iroquois sovereignty threatens to balkanize Canada, a strange comment from the genius of Meech Lake. It need not be so. The Iroquois trace their relationship with whites to the Two Row Wampum, a seventeenth-century treaty belt that shows Indians and Europeans travelling together down the same river, but each in their own boats. Most Iroquois seek an agreement in this spirit—a way to live as different nations side by side. They do not want to threaten Canada's sovereignty; they want Canada to stop threatening theirs. We are lucky this is all they ask. What would we do if they demanded full independence for the little territories they have left—the sort of independence enjoyed by small European nations such as San Marino? At twenty-four square miles, San Marino is smaller than several Iroquois reserves.

The sequence of events from which the Mohawk crisis has

emerged is sickeningly familiar. The so-called rule of law, used relentlessly as a tool to dispossess, repress, and divide the Indians, is finally met by men with guns in a corner. This then justifies the use of overwhelming force in the name of "civilization". It is the same pattern as the Cherokee Trail of Tears (1838-39) and the Wounded Knee massacre (1890). It is also familiar from Latin American countries such as Guatemala, where the army's main job is to keep on conquering the Indians.

In the late twentieth century it is no longer acceptable for European colonists to dominate the indigenous peoples of Africa and Asia. How much longer will the world find it acceptable for the whites of the Americas to do the same?

FOURTEEN

Outback

I'd felt Australia's magnetism when I was in Fiji in 1983, writing my second book. Australia is the United States of the South Pacific: an economic powerhouse; a neo-colonial presence. The tiny island countries hear her breathing over the horizon: Australian accents on the airwaves, Australian electrical sockets, fragments of dialect, and great trading firms like Carpenters and Burns Philp with a branch everywhere you go.

It was only about four hours by air from Fiji to Sydney, but I couldn't afford the time or the money to go there. Australia's sheer bulk was daunting: an island the size of a continent. I'd met many Aussies in odd spots around the world. When they left home they made the most of it, travelling for two or three years until their cash or their health ran out. They were serious about leaving; I felt I should be equally serious about going there. Six months seemed a minimum.

I'd wanted to go for as long as I remember. I think I sensed as a child that one day I'd leave England. Australia was always the first place that came to mind. I imagined it in tones of red and yellow, a bleached and glaring sunshine that I must have picked up from travel films and books like Nevil Shute's *On the Beach.* As it turned out, I ended up in Canada, a land of white and grey; but every winter, usually in February (by far the cruellest month), I'd remember that sunny glare and think about moving on to Oz. I mentioned this long desire to Jack McIver over lunch—in the heady days when magazines had money. He sent me there for *Destinations* in 1989.

I came back wishing I'd discovered Australia twenty years ago. It seemed to have everything Canada had, without the brutal climate. It was happily isolated, far from God and far from the United States. There, on that big island, a distinctive culture had emerged, with its own language and its own irreverent gaze under a light so much clearer and more intense than I'd imagined.

I GREW UP in Britain, but part of me had always been Australian. Australia was Britain's frontier. It was where you went if you fell out with your parents, lost your job, left your wife, or simply got suffocated by the stale proprieties of little England. The only time I got good marks in geography was when I had to do an "Australia Project". My twelve-year-old hand stencilled GOLD, URANIUM, OPALS on a country thirty times bigger than my own. I cut out pictures of a golden land beneath a hard, clear light. I imagined the smell of gum trees and the spoor of strange marsupials. Then I turned to the louring sky outside the classroom window and smelled the boiled cabbage we would have, again, for lunch; and I knew that Australia was where I'd go when I failed my exams.

The Australia I imagined had no schools or towns. It was invoked by one word: *Outback.* Perhaps I knew, even then, that the Outback is a country of the mind. It waits at the fringe of civilization, where the surveyed web spun by the coastal cities runs out of thread. Its border depends on your definition of the wild. To Sydneysiders it might be somewhere beyond the Blue Mountains that bulge under the western sky. To an Adelaider it starts up the railway line, near Port Augusta, where the irrigated wheatland gives way to bush country and salt-pans shown disingenuously on maps as Lake Torrens and Lake Eyre. The Woomera Prohibited Area near these "lakes" is most certainly Outback, even though it bears the stamp of Aussie humour and twentieth-century madness: a lavatory bowl stands at ground zero of a British nuclear test, and radioactive dust still drifts across the saltbush and the spinifex.

Thirty years later I was there, heading north by train from Adelaide to Alice Springs. I'm not fond of trains, but I'd imagined this one to be a romantic affair of iron, mahogany, and brass. It was called the Ghan, after Afghani camel drivers who plied this route a century ago; it turned out to be a pale cigar tube of aluminium, stainless steel, and bleached-oak formica. You couldn't control the air-conditioning and you couldn't open a window. My cabin measured about six feet by three. The wall opposite my seat was dominated by a fold-away steel toilet as daunting in appearance and operation as the zero-gravity contraption in Stanley Kubrick's *2001*.

I fled to watch the dawn from the bar car, where I found one occupant stranded from the night before. Bruce MacIntyre had eyebrows like two fuzzy white caterpillars. His strawberry nose had been marinated for a good many years in bourbon, which he had been drinking with Coke until the small hours. The caterpillars buckled as he squinted at the sunrise.

Yesterday's dusk had fallen on a landscape like the prairies—great wheatfields in grim, logical squares—except that roads and creeks were lined with gums instead of poplars. Their bark was swirled with glutinous patterns of grey, olive, and mauve, like battleship camouflage. But the sun rose on red earth and gaunt vegetation mirrored in pools of floodwater. I've seen deserts elsewhere, but nothing had prepared me for this. It didn't seem to belong to planet Earth. Not a single plant species was familiar, and the vibrant brick-red soil looked exactly like those pictures sent back from the surface of Mars.

"The Territory," MacIntyre said, nodding at the window.

"Outback?" I said. "Would you call this part the Outback?"

"The whole bloody thing is Outback, mate. 'Cept Darwin City, I spose."

I'd asked a stupid question. I turned to the window and for once saw something I could recognize: a windmill, idling.

"What kind of stock would they have here? Sheep?"

"No, not sheep 'ere, mate. Cattle more like. Sheep's dahn sahth." MacIntyre was surprisingly bright for a man who had been drinking bourbon and Coke.

"How can they live? There's no soil."

"Course there's soil! All it wants is water." He pronounced it in the Cockney way, with a glottal stop in the middle. "Give it wau'er—grow like a bastard. Look at them trees—buggers are lush now 'cause they've 'ad rine."

As the sun climbed, it woke the desert colours: every green from reseda to jade to avocado; crimson flowers like Indian paintbrush; patches of raw soil so bright I mistook them for blooms.

MacIntyre took out a pipe, tapped it on the door, and started to fill it.

"Them Asians could live here. Grow their own food. Work 'ard. They'd live 'igh." He meant boat people and Hong Kong Chinese. It seemed a generous thought, given that Australians of his generation once feared the yellow peril. In this empty continent, not far from the world's most crowded nations, it wasn't hard to understand that old fear, and to see that it was really guilt: Asia's millions overrunning the whites as thoroughly as the whites had overrun the Aboriginals.

I looked again at the desert. The country had been the same for hours. I'd seen no people, no vehicles, no cattle, no more windmills, not a single kangaroo. The only human presence was the railway itself. Put someone from Hong Kong here, I thought, and he'd go mad in a day.

In Alice Springs every bookshop and newsstand sells Nevil Shute's *A Town Like Alice*, less than ten pages of which are actually about Alice. His title is a bit like the town's River Todd, which can go years without a drop. It was winter here, south of the equator, and central Australia felt like a prairie fall. You could live like a lizard on the dazzling light, but the dry air held no warmth. When darkness came the mercury sank to zero and I shivered in my cotton sweater. The Ghan had arrived at noon. Alice, I'd observed, was a prim town of 26,000 people, three traffic lights, and a pedestrian mall. Bungaloid growth stretched off into the bush. Alice ran on government jobs and tourism. Alice was a town like Whitehorse.

I went to a steakhouse and washed down dinner with Red Back, a beer named after a venomous spider dreaded for its habit of lurking under backyard "dunny" seats. Afterwards I sat at the bar, trying to numb myself sufficiently before walking back to my hotel.

"G'day."

"G'day."

"You the new journo in town? They told me to look out for ya. Denham's the nime." Denham held out a relaxed hand. He said he was from a place called Bendigo, in the state of Victoria. His passion for Australian Rules football had cost him two front teeth. But his face, which seemed always in repose, was a natural smile. It showed the contentment of a man who has found a place and a life that suit him perfectly.

"Media co-ordinator and professional drunk," he added,

patting pockets forgetfully. "Know what I done? Just left me wallet behind, that's what. And me propaganda."

"No worries. Have a drink."

Denham's smile lit up: "A man's not a camel!"

"Camels I've seen. But I've been in Australia a week now, and I've yet to see a kangaroo."

"You drivin'?"

"Picking up a car tomorrow."

"Usually the first roo you see is the one that comes through yer windscreen. Take it easy after dark, mate. That's when they come out."

He asked me how long I had and ran his finger over my map. "Don't waste yer time in The Alice, get out and see the country—that's what yer 'ere for." His finger stabbed at a place in the middle of nowhere called Wallara Ranch, on the back route to Ayers Rock. "Wallara's a great pub. It's been known to roar." The finger circled and his tone grew wistful: "Ah, the brine demmage. The brine demmage you can suffer there."

By this time a certain amount of brain damage seemed likely at the steakhouse. If I was going to get out of "The Alice" tomorrow, I had to leave. Stars filled a sky that seemed much closer than usual, and the air smelt of eucalyptus smoke. I went back to my room, flipped on the TV, and watched a young Aboriginal woman read the news. Aboriginals run Imparja, the Territory's television network. It's a measure of how things have changed since the federal government recognized their title to large tracts of land in the 1970s. This was something new in Australia. The British had never acknowledged that the world's biggest penal colony had any prior inhabitants. Australia was *terra nullius*, empty land. There were no treaties, not even broken ones, with the "Blackfellow", because officially he did not exist. But there were massacres and smallpox and poisoned waterholes.

I'd seen Aboriginals in town, wandering uncertainly on prim

sidewalks, as if expecting to be chased away, their skin a carbon-paper black that absorbs all light, and what you notice are large soft eyes beneath heavy brows, eyes that seem sad and yet forgiving. Down in the dry bed of the Todd, they slept off their drinking and despair—small knots of ragged cowboy clothes, print dresses, woollen "beanies" and felt hats among the chalky trunks of the ghost gums.

The stink of air freshener in my car was so powerful I suspected it concealed something nasty, but then I'd smelled this same air-spray in most of the rooms I'd stayed in. It was another of those quaint relics of the 1950s that survive in Australia, like lace curtains and Vegemite, a spread that looks and tastes like a mixture of soy sauce and putty. I opened all the windows, turned the heater on full blast, and headed north up the Stuart Highway, named after John Stuart, who crossed the continent from south to north in 1861-62. Until then central Australia was thought to hold an inland sea, but Stuart found that the rivers ended in salt-pans and there had been no sea here for millions of years.

"Yew'd love Australia," an Australian told me years ago in an Earls Court pub. "There's nothing better than drahvin' out in the desert on a Saturday, drinkin' beer, and throwin' the cans out the window. Man! What a sense of freedom!" I was on open highway and I knew what he meant. The verges were impossibly red, as if someone had sprayed pigment on each side of the road. Primeval trees and bushes stretched away to infinity. There was no other traffic and, best of all, no speed limit. I was riding a black asphalt gunbarrel aimed at a tiny notch on the horizon. The white line seemed to pull me along. I peeled open a Fosters and grew a heavy foot.

At times like this, years of conditioning slip away and you begin running movies in your head. The needle hits 160kph (100 miles an hour: the magic ton), 170, 180, and suddenly this isn't a deodorized Toyota sedan—it's a V-8 Holden with a drum of nitro in the trunk, and you're the Road Warrior.

I don't know how long this reverie lasted, but eventually I saw something big and blue coming straight for me in the middle of the road. The space between us vanished in a second. I ran my wheels onto the dirt. Sixty-two wheels of road train went by like a Tokyo express. Ah yes, Denham had warned me about those: a big Mack, three trailers, and a Rasputin-bearded "truckie" living on lager and little white pills. My foot came off the pedal and the desert slowed down. I began to notice hazards. Every few miles there were dead cattle, some bloated like sex dolls, others as flat as bearskin rugs; the older ones were just a few bones and a brown stain on the dirt.

I was about to turn back to Alice when my eye was caught by what looked like a gypsy camp near the road. A limp brown flag hung above an old bus covered in Aboriginal motifs; there were shanties and lean-tos made of branches and corrugated iron. A sign said *Take Your Stock Route, Give Us Back Our Country.* Another amounted to a succinct history of Australia: *Station Owners 3 Generations, Us Mob 40,000 Years.*

I drove up to the first shack and met a white man with a socket wrench in his hand. He had a thin beard, blue eyes, and dusty glasses; he wore jeans, an old grey sweater, and suspicion. I told him I was a journo and he put the wrench down. Des Carne was from Sydney—he'd come up to the Territory a few years ago and got involved in Aboriginal land rights. "I've made this me home," he said, squinting at the desert where the afternoon light spilled through a gap between the horizon and the overcast. He said he was an adviser, with the Department of Aboriginal Affairs. He also had a personal connection: he'd married an elder's daughter. "You want to know what we're doing? It's a long story. Got an hour?"

Carne talked of land claims and conflicting interests. About 30 per cent of the Northern Territory's population is Aboriginal—

the highest proportion in Australia—and a comparable area of land was returned by the federal government to "traditional owners" shortly before the Territory became self-governing in 1976. Of course there were problems. Crown land was given back, but cattle stations—ranches that own or lease thousands of square miles of the best land—were scarcely touched. The Aboriginals are highly diverse, speaking many languages and belonging to different kin groups. Some did well; others were left out.

"Our protest here," Carne said, "directly concerns about a hundred and twenty adults—the people in this camp—who are trying to get a few square kilometres that they can call home excised from a cattle station. But it also concerns thousands of others in the same boat."

It was five o'clock by now. The sun gathered itself like a teardrop and slipped from behind the cloud. The desert changed from sombre greys and greens to gold. "Come on," Carne said. "I'll show you around." Under an iron "humpie" (a lean-to) sat an old man with rheumy eyes and a bandaged hand. He was warming his face in the sun and a tin of meat in his fire. Carne introduced him as Henry Turner; we shook hands. I felt the texture of the bandages and noticed he was very shy. Beyond was a small clearing with some children playing beneath an acacia tree. They were laughing and speaking their own language, Arrernte. Carne pointed to the bus with the cheerful paint job. "How do you like that? That's our school." The designs looked abstract to me, dots and squiggles arranged in swirling patterns, but to an Aboriginal each shape symbolizes plants and animals and things we have no words for: a complete iconography of the world. In Sydney I'd seen a photograph of a BMW painted like this by Michael Jagamara Nelson—a surreal image of Australia's two solitudes. As art, the painting on the bus was less impressive, but it was an eloquent attempt to humanize the inhuman.

Silas Turner, Carne's father-in-law, was standing beside a

larger shack near the bus. He stood tall and very straight in a navy felt jacket and dark stetson with an orange hatband. He looked like a black sergeant from the American Civil War. The two spoke in Arrernte for a while, and then Carne told me more. Their strategy was to occupy this stock route (a mile-wide right of way for cattle drives) which could in theory be returned to Aboriginals. They did not want this particular stretch of land, but they were hoping to swap it with the rancher for the piece they did want.

Like all Aboriginal clans, these people belong to a certain "country"—an area where every rock, tree, and waterhole has deep religious meaning going back to the primordial Dreamtime. At such sacred sites throughout Australia the heroes of the Dreamtime—be they kangaroos, lizards, or honey ants—sang themselves and the world into existence. The Dreamtime heroes are totemic ancestors of woman and man. An Aboriginal's country is thus her Eden, her Mecca, her family tree, her cathedral, and her tomb.

Unfortunately, it isn't always easy for today's Aboriginals to prove such things in white courts, which, according to Carne, are seldom sympathetic: "The Territorial government is still a colonial one. They defend the landed gentry, the pastoralists. They think the federal government went too far. They'd like to keep the Blackfellow in his place. And that usually means keeping him in town."

Aboriginals and ranchers had for years lived in a kind of symbiosis—unequal but interdependent on the same land. Aboriginal stockmen drove the cattle across vast reaches of Outback which only they knew. The ranchers drilled wells and supplied water and other essentials in a changing world. Then, about thirty years ago, it got out that Aboriginal workers were being paid far less than white ones. An outcry was raised and a well-meaning law was passed. If there had been no alternative, ranchers might have kept their stockmen and paid them more. But mechanization was cheaper. The motorbike and aeroplane replaced the black cowboy; thousands were forced off the land and into towns like Alice.

I don't know how many times I've heard that old Australian song "Tie Me Kangaroo Down, Sport". For the first time a verse of it made sense:

Let me Abos go loose, Bruce,
Let me Abos go loose.
They're of no further use, Bruce,
Let me Abos go loose.

I wanted to see that great red monolith, Ayers Rock, Australia's petrified heart. I drove south from Alice for an hour or so, then left the pavement and turned west along a road that was merely a strip of red sand kept free of vegetation by a grader. I saw no other vehicles. I felt marooned by the laconic signs: Wallara 99; Kings Canyon 199. Those who think the prairies are empty should come here. One grain elevator every half-hour is a suburb compared to this. In days of driving I saw: no Aboriginals, no ranchers, no kangaroos, no camels, one dingo, one wedge-tailed eagle, two emus (a pair), and maybe six cows—not counting dead ones. But this emptiness was an illusion. Feral camels are so numerous that Australia exports meat and breeding stock to Arabia, kangaroos have to be culled, dingos have been known to snatch babies from campgrounds, and Aboriginals still follow their "dreaming tracks", the unseen web of history, myth, and genealogy that exists in their minds and souls (and which Bruce Chatwin popularized in *The Songlines*). The desert does not give up its secrets easily to strangers. The emptiness was not real; it was my ignorance. And most of what I did see I could not describe. I had entered another creation, to which I did not belong and for which I had no words. I was out of place and time. English has no good names for these trees and bushes that were old when the dinosaurs were young.

The desert oaks are not oaks; the corkwoods are not corks; the desert poplar is not a poplar. Australia is flat, but the flatness is not the work of glaciers (which were still scraping over Europe and America a mere 12,000 years ago). This flatness is the work of nothing but wind, sun, rain, and frost. And time. Aeons of time. The oldest rocks in the world are here, and they are almost as old as the earth itself—more than four billion years. Australia is a great fragment of the old supercontinent, Gondwanaland; and while other fragments became new continents with new lives—new mountains, new volcanoes—nothing much happened here but time. So much time that Australia's mountains turned to dust.

I drove on, past Wallara Ranch, to Kings Canyon; past verges lined with ruby dock and paddy melon, past silver grasslands heaving in the wind. Of course, Australia's climate changed over the ages—the inland seas evaporated, the topsoil blew away, the eucalypt forests crept to the fringes of the continent—but all this happened so gradually that life could adapt. At the bottom of Kings Canyon, beside deep crevices where pools of dark water survive throughout the dry season, I saw cycads and palms whose ancestors grew in jungles and on vanished shores. There are burrowing frogs that hold water in their bodies for years; there are aquatic scorpions that fly when their pools disappear; there's a lizard, called the thorny devil, with catchment areas for dew all over its back. And the birds—the emerald green lorikeets and red-and-grey galahs, the white corellas and the green-and-yellow Port Lincoln parrots—these too are jungle dwellers who stayed on in the central desert because it dried up so slowly that they failed to notice.

Wallara Ranch is a watering hole for less adapted life forms. I got back there at dusk and checked into one of the best rooms—a clean but Spartan Atco trailer. After a camel T-bone, I repaired to the bar, where I hoped to witness, if not experience, some of the "brine demmage" so fondly recalled by Denham. You cannot enjoy Australia without enjoying pubs. Australia drinks more alcohol per capita than any other English-speaking nation. In Sydney I'd drunk at the Hero of Waterloo, which claims to be the oldest pub in the land. I was persuaded when I saw the cellar: a dungeon, complete with iron shackles, where sturdy lads who got too pissed were held for sale to navy press gangs. To sit in the Hero's nineteenth-century drinking chairs—like pews with arms—was to understand the sacramental role of alcohol in Australia. It would be a formidable task to work out how many gallons of beer and rum, on that very spot, have been poured down the gizzard of Oz.

Wallara makes no claim to antiquity, though it is mentioned in *A Town Like Alice.* The bar was already full and the plywood floor awash with beer. GONDWANALAND was painted on a door. Young men in singlets and shorts were milling round a billiard table, jabbing their cues in the air like tribesmen at a spear dance. Hanging above their heads was an array of underpants—forfeited by heavy losers.

"See that bloke there?" Jane the barmaid handed me a Fourex (XXXX) and nodded at a player with a leonine head and a gut like a deckchair in a wind. "He was propping up the bar in nothing but his shirt and a smile last time. Bloody oath!" The walls were covered in postcards and droll stickers like this: *I hate this bloody job. Who do you have to sleep with to get the sack?* A bulldozer driver from New Zealand—a Maori whom everyone called Kiwi—was strumming a guitar and singing dubious songs at the top of his voice: "Two pist... Two pist... Two pistols in yer 'and...."

Underpants came over and belched. "Scuse. Shout you a beer? Whatcher 'avin?" I drained my Fourex and decided to try VB (Victoria Bitter). Underpants was with the telephone company, stringing lines through the Outback, a job that gave him "a thirst you could take a picture of." His mate was wearing mirror sunglasses and a gimme cap that said *Share Your Banana with Me.* More introductions and where-are-you-froms; I shouted a round. Underpants stood back and said: "So yore 'riginally a Pom, are yer?" I thought: that does it, Australians don't like Poms.

"My ancestors. . . ." He was stabbing my chest with a finger. "My ancestors were chosen to come out here by some of the *finest* judges in England."

At this point I thought it a good idea to include two elderly ladies sitting at a corner table in the conversation. They were from Adelaide, Emmeline and Vale. Vale had lost her husband not long before this trip and she was pining. Even the wildlife made her think of him.

"You get possums round 'ere?" she asked Underpants. She drank a VB straight down. "I can't bear to see a possum. We had one on our station. Me and Bert had a thousand square miles, you know." She took out a hanky and dabbed at her rouged cheeks. "There was this possum lived in a tree we called the possum tree. How my Bert loved that possum! When Bert was goin'—he knew it, see—he said to me, 'Vile. That's where you can scatter me ashes. Under the possum tree.'"

"Nuther round, Jane love!" Underpants called.

"Comin' up."

"Beauty!"

"Well, the time came—cheers everyone!—and I went down to the possum tree with Bert in the urn. And there was that little face, up on a branch, looking down at me, and I thought, *he knows. He knows,* that possum does." Vale was sobbing again; Underpants stepped into the breach.

"When I go, mate," he said with a wink at Jane, "I want 'em to take me ashes and scatter 'em dahn on the beach. That way the crabs can get a dose of me for a change, instead of me gettin' a dose of the crabs."

Next morning I had that brittle, eidetic clarity that sometimes follows a rough night. The oaks, mulgas, and coolibahs stood out from sand like powdered blood. The desert seemed to glow, and it wasn't as empty as before. I saw flocks of crested pigeons—odd little birds with punky black tufts on their heads—and when I stopped to look at them they took flight with a metallic whistling from their wings. I drove south on dirt for a while, then turned west on the paved highway to Ayers Rock. I passed about two or three vehicles per hour—heavy traffic—usually a Toyota 4WD with jerrycans on the roof and New South Wales plates. Every so often there was a rest area with a picnic table, a rubbish barrel, and a water tank. SAVED WATER SAVES LIVES: TAKE ONLY WHAT YOU NEED.

Grasslands and desert oaks gave way to a rippled country of dunes sparsely covered with dryland bushes. (Australia has no cacti, which are native only to the Americas.) It had rained recently, and nearly all were in bloom—brilliant umbelliferous white flowers like baby's breath, yellow lupin-like grevillea blossoms, scarlets, purples, and mauves among blackened skeletons from bushfires—all embroidered on the magenta sand.

A dingo, huge, loped across the road. Then I saw something more astonishing, a mountain: Mount Conner, a mesa surrounded by talus slopes. Half an hour later Ayers Rock rose like a moon on the horizon.

Uluru, the Aboriginals call it. It is a mountain all of a piece, one stone more than five miles in circumference, a thousand feet high, and who knows how deep. Nothing on earth resembles this elephantine monolith rising abruptly from the plain. Oddest of all is the lack of erosional debris at its base. Uluru's walls drop straight into the ground, as if it were floating in the desert, as if an asteroid had fallen to earth and tidily buried itself to the waist.

As the rock comes closer, a third eminence rises beyond it: the Olgas, a huddle of domes like the stone helmets of a war memorial.

This is the extraordinary thing: here in the very centre of the continent are these three small mountains, all that is left of a range worn away to dust. And yet they are not in the least alike. Mount Conner would fit in the American Southwest. The Olgas might have bubbled from the earth. And Uluru, the world's largest monolith, seems to have dropped from the sky.

I climbed a dune and sat to watch cloud shadows drifting across Uluru's surface. The stone blushed, frowned darkly, blushed again, and smiled in pink. Uluru has always been sacred to Aboriginals. When a national park was created here, and the tourist clutter removed to Yulara, this land was deeded back to its traditional owners (with a proviso that others be allowed to visit).

I waited until evening for the climb. It's about an hour's walk, far steeper and more strenuous than one imagines from the ground. But the greatest surprise is the texture and form of the rock. The smooth contours seen from a distance resolve into a complex and baffling sculpture: ridges, valleys, caves, and hollows, folded and sinuous as if the surface were petrified skin. Set here and there like cabochons are hollows filled with water—cobalt pools of sky. And when it rains, the rock erupts in waterfalls.

From the top I could just make out Mount Conner, on the horizon fifty miles away and fading quickly. To the west and nearer, the Olgas were swallowing the sun. People came in twos and threes and sat by the small cairn that marks the summit. Nobody spoke above the wind.

FIFTEEN

Kangaroo

Some time after returning from Australia, I got a letter from the distinguished and dauntingly energetic George Woodcock, asking if I had anything suitable for a collection of writers' incidents to be called *The Great Canadian Anecdote Contest.* His idea was to edit a humorous book to help support Canada India Village Aid, a charity he and his wife had founded ten years before, which drills wells and provides basic services in many parts of rural India. "Surely," he wrote, "there's an unused diamond from somewhere in your travels."

Well, there *was* one that came to mind. Possibly a zircon, if I'd had it assayed. But anecdotes must be taken at face value.

I WAS SETTLING the day's dust with a chilled tube at Wallara—that little bar deep in the Outback with a billiard table and a ceiling festooned with the underpants of those who wagered their shorts and lost—when in walked Jurgen and Floyd: two men with prairie accents and one jacket between them; two men visibly shaken.

They were realtors from a place called Product, Saskatchewan. The Outback, they said, hadn't intimidated them till now. They liked plenty of driving and plenty of sky. Mountains and trees spoiled the view. The thousand-mile asphalt bootlace tying Alice Springs to Adelaide hadn't seemed much hotter than the Trans-Canada in August. But unlike home, it had no speed limit. Floyd had been driving, and as fast as he liked: 190, 200.... What was that in miles per hour? The trip was his treat, thanks to a big sale, and he was determined to enjoy it. Each fall for twenty-seven years, he and Jurgen had stalked moose and drunk beer together in the muskeg. They had beer with them in the car—nothing unlawful about that here—a couple of dozen sitting in a cooler like ammunition in a clip. Every half-hour, Floyd's hand strayed behind the seat and pried loose another one.

"Wasn't gettin drunk or nothin," he said. The beer was just to keep his mouth wet. The desert air, breathing in the windows like a dragon, sucked the alcohol from his pores as fast as he could get it down. He was thinking about moose: he'd miss them this year. Some people said a camel was a horse designed by a committee, but surely they were wrong. It had to be a moose.

Moose don't hop, Floyd almost had time to remind himself, when a brownish shape leapt from a clump of mulga bush. He hit the brakes but at that speed the car had the momentum of a train; animal and vehicle were destined to meet.

The impact woke Jurgen from a snooze. The two got out. They looked at the steam escaping from the radiator, at the soft white fur on the belly of the weird creature lying on the road. Funny how the Aussies shortened everything. This wasn't a kangaroo; it was just a roo. And the roo bars, intended for trouble like this, hadn't done their job.

"So Jurgen says to me, 'You grab his tail and I'll grab his paws, and we'll haul him out the goddam way.'"

They pushed the car into the meagre shade of a desert oak and began a long wait. They couldn't sit down because of ants. They couldn't sit in the car for heat. The sun lowered itself and blasted away their shade.

Floyd sank another, then ran his hand over a meaty face. He continued: "'Tell you what,' Jurgen says to me when our beer's all gone. 'Let's get some pictures of this fella for our better halves back home.'" They grasped the dead roo by its tail, thick and limp like a bell rope, and dragged it over to the car. The roo was heavier than it looked, but they managed to prop it up against the grille with its fine head lolling on its chest like a drunken girl's. Floyd took pictures of Jurgen with his arm around the narrow tawny shoulders and his baseball cap perched between the ears. The cap said PRODUCT: LAND OF PLENTY. Jurgen took some of Floyd. Then he got his jacket—a purple nylon jacket with PRODUCT REALTY emblazoned over the pocket in orange lettering—and put it on the kangaroo. The effect, I gathered, was Peter Rabbit on heroic scale.

Floyd and Jurgen stepped back to admire their tableau, and as they did so, the butt of their humour raised its head and regarded them with dreamy eyes. Then, before the two men could react, the kangaroo shook itself and hopped off into the desert. The baseball cap fell to the ground. But the purple nylon jacket, containing Jurgen's passport and travellers' cheques, disappeared into an Outback sunset.

"Good thing we got the pictures," said Floyd, signalling for another beer. "American Express might be sticky with a refund."

SIXTEEN

Return to the Islands

The idea of going to Fiji to write a book came to me in 1983, soon after *Cut Stones and Crossroads* was accepted for publication by Viking. A friend of mine, J. Rod Vickers—we had been students together at Calgary—returned from a long archaeological project in the interior of the main island, Viti Levu. Of course one expected to hear about Fiji's obvious attractions—warm beaches, coral reefs, tropical forests. I was more surprised by his descriptions of the people.

I'd heard vaguely about what happened to the Hawaiians and the Maoris; like the American Indians, they had become marginalized and disoriented, powerless minorities in their own homes. But Rod insisted that the same thing had not happened in Fiji. Native Fijians had managed to keep their way of life, their social structure, and they wielded real political clout through the ballot box and their traditional chiefs, hereditary leaders whose pedigrees went back to when Fiji was an archipelago of warring chiefdoms, dreaded by seamen as the "Cannibal Isles". Though colonized by Britain from 1874 to 1970, Fijians held no hatred for their former colonizers. In fact they were sorry to see the Union Jack pulled down. They'd managed to become Methodists without losing faith in their own culture. They travelled the world as sportsmen and soldiers but always returned to the village. They lived as subsistence farmers, yet read newspapers in Fijian. In short, they had adapted to the modern world on their own terms. They were also the pleasantest, most self-assured people Rod had ever met. And at the bottom of all this lay the fortunate anomaly that, unlike most indigenous peoples around the world, they had not been deprived of their ancestral lands.

A price had been paid, of course. In order to spare Fijians, the British had brought indentured labourers from India. They suffered on the sugar estates, and their descendants form about half the population today. When I was in Fiji in 1983 someone told me, "If the Indians ever win an election here, there'll be a military coup." It seemed far-fetched at the time, even though I knew that the two main races kept to themselves and tended to support opposing parties. When the British went home to their own islands, they had left behind a convoluted electoral system intended to make sure that neither race could dominate the other. In practice, the Fijian party had a slight advantage, though this was balanced by the economic strength of Indian planters and businessmen. The Fijians also had the army, a legacy of the Second World War, when thousands of Fijians—but very few Fiji Indians—had volunteered to fight the Japanese. I knew that this small but effective force (which often serves with the U.N.) was the Fijians' trump card, their ultimate veto. But the Fiji I saw in 1983 was a tranquil place. I foresaw no need for *coups d'état.* Neither did anyone else—except for that one informant. I left his remark out of my book, and soon regretted it.

On Fiji Islands was published in 1986. In April 1987, an Indian-dominated coalition won Fiji's general elections. Within weeks, Colonel Sitiveni Rabuka, an athletic Fijian with views as taut and conservative as his trim moustache, had overthrown the government.

Two years later, on my way back from Australia, I made a short visit to the islands.

EVEN AT THREE O'CLOCK in the morning, when my plane landed, I could tell that things had changed. The old immigration hall, with its naïve mural and slow, smiling officer, was gone. Instead there were two officers who did not smile and who looked up my name in a computer. I wondered if *On Fiji Islands* and its author were *non grata*: this could be a very short visit or a very long stay. But my passport was handed back—still no smile—and I was in. I retrieved my suitcase and walked stiffly past two soldiers in the customs hall. They were black and burly, built like Olympian heroes, and wore the crisp moustache favoured by Fijian troops.

There'd been some bother at the airport during the coup. An Indian carrying dynamite had wanted to go to Libya, but his travel plans had ended with a blow to the head from a flight engineer wielding a whisky bottle. Apart from that, Fiji hadn't seen much violence by the standards of other ethnically divided nations: no deaths, a few fistfights, some shops looted, some Indians beaten up, and a *lovo*—a cannibal oven-pit—dug on the parliament lawn by young "warriors" with a darkly historical sense of humour. When things settled down, the press called it the Friendly Coup.

Nadi Town, near the international airport at the west end of Viti Levu, the big island, is mainly an Indian place. The land is flat and dry, parcelled up into sugarcane fields. Casuarinas shade the narrow roads, and here and there on the uplands are plantings of Caribbean pine. The air smells of woodsmoke, molasses, and frangipani; cows wander about with an insolence born of their holiness to Hindus. I wanted to get to the wet side of Viti Levu, a hundred miles to the east, where rainforest sweeps down from the central mountains and laps at the suburbs of Suva, the capital. I rented a tiny car with a three-cylinder engine, a few dents, and a musty smell from upholstery slowly rotting in the tropical air.

I hadn't gone far along the Queen's Road—the main route around the south coast of the island—when a man in bell-bottoms and a T-shirt flagged me down. He owned a taxi, which had broken down, and needed a lift to the capital for parts. I could tell he was a Hindu from his keychain—an icon of Ganesh, the elephant-headed god of prosperity. His name was Vishnu. Thinking he might want to bend a stranger's ear on political grievances, I asked about the troubles.

"Oh, that all died down. Nobody care about that now." He sounded evasive.

"But thousands of Indian people left?" I said.

"Those with the means. We can't all leave. Quite a few come back. OK, we have racism here, but not like racism in the white countries! Australia, Canada, New Zealand—maybe they let us vote there but treat us terrible, you know! Nobody worrying here now. Just get on with sleeping, eating, and vorking. Even the Sunday shutdown—that end too. Now buses, taxis, restaurants, all open."

Fijians are, among other things, devout Methodists who added missionary puritanism to the ancient Polynesian edicts of *tabu*; the coup leaders had imposed regulations against working on Tabu Day, the day of the Lord. But this revived sabbatarianism, aimed at non-Christians, was almost as unpopular with young Fijians, who enjoy a good rugby match and a few beers on Sunday afternoons.

"You know, I get lazy," Vishnu said. "Before the coup, I vorking very hard. Seven days a week. Like a crazy man! Now, after two years not vorking on Sundays, I don't *vant* to!" He seemed astonished by his own confession, then grew more philosophical. "But now I think it's good. More time for family and vife."

There was an anti-smoking campaign in Fiji. Along the road were billboards saying DON'T USE THESE COFFIN NAILS. But I had entered the country beneath a welcoming Rothmans arch, and every picturesque village we passed had its name done in silly dancing letters above the familiar majuscule of Benson & Hedges. On a bus shelter someone had scrawled ARMY OUT.

All this time I'd been nagged by the feeling that I'd met Vishnu, or someone very like him, before. Then I had it: the doorman at my uncle's stockbroking firm in the City. He had the same south Indian looks and manner—very dark, with big glossy eyes and an earnest brow. I'd never learned his real name. The young jobbers called him Mahatma Coat.

"And you sir?" Vishnu asked. "What line are you?" The subject of work was still uppermost in Vishnu's mind. Subscription to the capitalist dream—a suburban bungalow and a car—is one of the things that distinguishes Fiji Indians from indigenous Fijians, who prefer to live in communal villages scattered throughout the moody hills and forests.

"I write."

"Tell me please sir. How much money you get from writing?"

I said it took time to become established.

"But some fellows," said Vishnu. "I hear some fellows writing and writing and not successful. Even after years! And then all that vorking and vorking. . . ." He sighed and shook his head in incomprehension as much as sympathy. "So much vastage of time and using up of brain."

Suva showed signs of the economic slowdown that had followed the coup. Streets, shops, cars, were less neat and prosperous than I remembered. The Grand Pacific Hotel, once a haven of colonial elegance, hadn't seen a lick of paint in years. I stayed there one night and decided to go to an island I hadn't visited before.

It was a bumpy hour in a light plane to Taveuni; beside me sat a stout Fijian businessman reading *Na Tui*, a newspaper in the native language. He was dressed formally in jacket, tie, and *sulu*—the Fijian knee-length kilt—below which his stocky calves were bare. Small planes made him nervous, he admitted, but he had important business in Taveuni's only town. Tomasi Nawaqatabu (in English his last name would be Holy Canoe) owned a bookshop in Suva and dabbled in real estate. He said that more Fijians were in business now that so many prosperous Indians had joined the "brain drain". He winced after a patch of turbulence and patted his *embonpoint*. "Bad for my ulcer," he said, meeting my raised eyebrow. "Imagine! A Fijian with an ulcer!" He shook with laughter. "People think we just wait for the coconuts to fall, but nowadays we have to knock them down ourselves."

Taveuni, third- or fourth-largest of Fiji's 400 islands, is remote and less than a twentieth the size of Viti Levu. Steep volcanoes rise along its spine, attracting almost constant rainfall. Rain and the lava soil give it a thick pelt of rainforest with a fringe of plantations—coconuts, spices, and fruit—on the lower slopes.

I stared through scratched perspex at clouds and peaks. "When the weather is good," said Nawaqatabu, "Taveuni is one of the loveliest spots on earth."

Maravu Plantation, once a copra estate, now provides a South Seas idyll for a handful of discerning foreigners. There were eight *bures* (cabins) hidden among hibiscus, croton, and flamboyant bushes so lush they had to be cut back from walls and paths every month. Here locals worked and visitors idled. Signs on the palm trees said BEWARE OF FALLING NUTS. A cow was drinking from the swimming pool when I arrived.

Ormond Eyre, Maravu's owner, put a large punch in my hand and asked if I was the chap who'd written *On Fiji Islands.* "I'll give you a discount if you sign that for me before you go." He nodded at a well-stocked bookshelf containing a familiar spine.

"I liked that book," he added. "But I wish you'd said a bit more about us, the mixed people. Fiji isn't only Indians and Fijians." It was fair comment: the main racial split had absorbed me. I hadn't said much about the other groups—Europeans, Chinese, and Part-Europeans—who together form a small but influential percentage, a casting vote, as it were, in Fiji's dichotomy. You could see Ormond's dual ancestry in his strong build, the twilight of his skin, the clear grey eyes.

After dinner he took down a *tanoa,* a large wooden kava bowl, from a peg on the wall. He mixed an infusion of the mildly narcotic root that is Fiji's social and ceremonial drink, and we drank alternately from coconut-shell cups.

Ormond is a great-great-grandson of the first white man to cross Australia from east to west, Edward John Eyre, who left his name on a lake and a peninsula. Charles Eyre, the explorer's son, came to Fiji more than a century ago as a lands commissioner for the first British governor. His work led to the enshrining in law of native clan title to more than four-fifths of Fiji—a system that restricted the property opportunities of immigrants, whether white or Indian, but saved native Fijians from the dispossession suffered by their Polynesian cousins in Hawaii, New Zealand, and elsewhere. Charles married a highborn Fijian from Beqa and stayed in the islands for the rest of his life. Ormond scooped another cupful from the bowl. *Tanoas* come in many sizes and are usually round or, more rarely, shaped like a turtle. Ormond's was a turtle bowl; it was old and very fine.

"This is great-grandfather's *tanoa.* He was a trader for many years. Then he lost everything to his rivals in 1929."

"It's beautiful," I said.

He said: "You know Fiji—remember never to admire anything if you visit a Fijian house. By the rules of tradition they have to give a stranger anything he praises. People sometimes walk off with carvings that have been in the family for generations."

"I'm sorry," I said. "I forgot."

"No worries. When it comes to property I'm European. It can be useful being half and half." He laughed. "We have the same mix on our mother's side. A lady of the Verata chiefdom married an old seafarer named James Valentine." He held out another cup; I clapped in the ceremonial way before taking and draining it.

"The Fijians accept us because we cling to our *vasu*, our lineage. But I still hate filling in that landing card—the box where I have to put down 'Part-European'. Still, it's not as bad as Australia. When I wanted to live there the white Australia policy was still in force. I had to lean heavily on great-great-grandfather's name."

Ormond was born on Taveuni and had recently returned from years of exile. He had gone to school in New Zealand and then worked as an airline steward with Qantas, based in Australia, Italy, and England.

"I always knew I'd come back. When we emigrated to New Zealand—I must have been about twelve—I said to my parents, 'This is a great holiday but when are we going home?' They said, 'We're not going home, we're staying here.' I think they were worried about what might happen in Fiji after independence. I made a vow then that I'd come back to Taveuni one day. And I have." He smiled peacefully and looked around him. Wind agitated the palms and the thatch of the dining-room roof. A breeze came in, stirring the flowers on the tables.

Wicker chairs began to fill with other guests and one or two locals who enjoyed a regular sundowner at Ormond's bar. A gaunt Englishman who worked for the government was telling a tale about the day of the coup.

"There was a crazy rumour going around that I was a Russian spy." The Englishman drained his whisky. "Anyway, I'm looking out of my office window and I see a soldier with an assault rifle just across the street. He keeps sort of shifting around on his feet and looking my way. Then he crosses over, looking very sly, and comes right up to my window. I thought, this is it! They're going to take me away and lock me up." The Englishman paused dramatically, scooping a handful from a bowl of crisps.

"Know what the chap says? *Have you got a smoke!*"

"Fiji really lost its virginity that day," said Ormond. "You could call it our coming of age. Healthy in a way. If it hadn't happened then it would have happened later—perhaps much worse."

The foreign press, I remembered, had tended to see the events as a case of right and wrong—the overturning of democracy and imposition of something tantamount to "black apartheid". It wasn't that simple, of course. In Fijian eyes, independence from Britain had itself been a kind of coup—carried out mainly by Indians. At that time Fijians were outnumbered, and they feared that a majority voting system could destroy the treaty guarantees that had enabled them to preserve the fabric of their society through a century of British rule. And apart from the racial problem, other forces were at work within both main groups: Muslim versus Hindu; ancient rivalries among the native chiefdoms.

"They're still trying to work out a new constitution," the Englishman said. "The idea is to guarantee a certain number of parliamentary seats for Fijians. It probably won't be fair to all races, but I know a lot of Indians who'd rather put up with Fijian politics than the discrimination they face in so-called democracies elsewhere."

I said I'd heard the same thing.

"Fiji's an enigma at the moment," Ormond added. "But I can tell you one thing. The numbers are changing. Fijians now outnumber Indians by a few thousand. When that sinks in, perhaps there won't be any need for special guarantees."

Next morning I was awake before dawn. The Milky Way faded, and light began to nibble at the edge of the world. I walked down through the trees to the beach. A fresh but unfamiliar perfume lay on the still air. The sand was strewn with delicate brush-like blossoms that had fallen during the night from barringtonias along the shore. As the sky brightened, I could just make out their colours: a spray of fine white stamens shading to a deep pink with orange tips. They looked like the tailfeathers of a gorgeous bird. The Pacific, a smooth grey skin, was tugging lazily at a spit of black lava that had once flowed hissing and incandescent into the sea. Such natural violence, like the troubles of men, now seemed inconceivably remote.

Opposite, across a strait, lay the small islands of Rabi and Kioa with the long whaleback of Vanua Levu behind them. As I watched, clouds clinging to the mountains turned pink, and the tropical dawn bled suddenly across the sky. I put on flippers and mask and slipped into the water.

SEVENTEEN

Sex, Lies, and Escape

Through *On Fiji Islands*, I'd become friends with Rob Kay, connoisseur of warm places and author of the Lonely Planet guides to Fiji and Tahiti. Postcards would arrive from Bora Bora, Thailand, Bali, and other sybaritic spots around the world. Rob knew the U.S. agent for the *Aranui*, a Tahitian ship that carries a small number of passengers on its cargo route between Papeete and the Marquesas. The berths were comfortable and expensive, but the owners, eager for publicity, often made empty ones available to travel writers. "Anytime you and your wife would like a free cruise, let me know," he said. He sent us a brochure.

I was working flat out on *Stolen Continents*, trying to beat a deadline I could do nothing about: the book had to be ready for 1992, the five-hundredth anniversary of Columbus's voyage. Janice was in England on her own research. A year went by and there seemed to be no time to get away. One day it dawned on me: we were being offered a free cruise in the South Seas, and we weren't taking it. We were crazy.

I called Rob Kay. It looked as though I could finish my book, leave it with my publishers in Boston, and go off for two months while they did the final editing. I'd earned enough airline points for free tickets to Sydney, so we could see a bit of Fiji and Australia as well. Best of all, the two months would be February and March. When we got back, it would be spring.

Because of the free tickets, plans had to be laid well in advance and could not be changed. Of course, they went awry. I thought I'd finished the book; my editor didn't agree. When he heard I was about to leave for the Marquesas, he was dismayed. Slowly and reluctantly, I realized I would have to do what amounted to another draft. I would have to cancel the trip.

At this point Janice made it clear that cancelling the trip was out of the question. The word divorce was mentioned. She persuaded me that I was much too close to what I'd written to give it a fresh eye, to judge what was needed and what was not. For the book's sake, I *needed* two months in the South Seas. I told this to my publishers.

"Can't we even fax you along your route?" they said. I said I thought that would be difficult.

Off we went, and for two months I didn't think about my book at all. It was the best thing I could have done.

IT WAS SAID of John Major, when he surprised everyone (not least Margaret Thatcher) by ousting the Iron Lady, that he is the only man who ran away from the circus to become an accountant. Such is not the romance of escape. Many of us, mired in the soft, predictable life, dream of running to the ends of the earth. Nowadays few do so, partly because the earth is overrun. But it wasn't always so, and there are still one or two retreats. I would choose the Marquesas, the remotest large islands in the Pacific. The Marquesas have been good to writers.

The young Herman Melville jumped ship there in 1842 and afterwards wrote *Typee*, which made his name and, during his lifetime, outsold *Moby Dick*. Half a century later, a wry, tubercular Robert Louis Stevenson passed through on his way to Samoa. Paul Gauguin, artist and libertine, came to live and die. So, more recently, did Jacques Brel, a Belgian cross between Bob Dylan and Tom Jones.

"The Marquesas!" Melville cried, when told that his filthy and starving whaler would make a landfall there. "What strange visions of outlandish things.... Naked houris—cannibal banquets—groves of cocoa-nut—coral reefs—tattooed chiefs—and bamboo temples... savage woodlands guarded by horrible idols—*heathenish rites and human sacrifices*."

All his expectations would be met, except for coral reefs (the Marquesas are too rough and steep for them). His voyage had not been pleasant. Driven by poverty to join a whaling ship at twenty-two, Melville had been at sea a year and a half; for the past six months he'd seen no land at all. The provisions were gone: "Even the bark that once clung to the wood we use for fuel has been gnawed off and devoured by the captain's pig; and ... the pig himself has in turn been devoured." Now there was only one swine left—the captain—who ran his ship with "unmitigated tyranny", flogging any man who complained.

When the young Melville saw the beauty of Nuku Hiva, largest of the islands, and of the people who lived there, he made up his mind to desert—a decision that shaped his life. The subsequent adventure was the stuff of melodrama: capture by cannibals, a love affair with a native girl, glimpses of taboo rites in sacred groves where fearsome idols presided over heaps of human bones. Then came a hair's-breadth escape aboard another vile ship, ending in mutiny on the high seas and jail in Tahiti. When Melville at last got back to Massachusetts he had been gone four years. And he had enough material for a lifetime's writing.

His first book, telling of his time on Nuku Hiva, was so sensational, so outspoken on the vices of sailors and missionaries, that no American publisher would touch it. *Typee* was printed in England, by the firm of John Murray, which is still in business at the same London address. The sequel, *Omoo*, was less successful; his other books, even *Moby Dick*, were flops. For the rest of his life Melville made his living as a customs clerk.

A dozen great rocks—half of them inhabited—in the middle of the ocean hemisphere, the Marquesas are still hard to reach. Nearly 1,000 miles northeast of Tahiti, 2,500 southeast of Hawaii, and 3,000 west of South America, they are not *en route* to anywhere. They have no international air links, no hotels bigger than a guest house. One or two small planes fly between the larger islands and Papeete, Tahiti, capital of French Polynesia. And there's a tramp steamer, locally known as the "ghost ship" because of its rare and capricious appearances. The only other way (apart from private yacht) is by the *Aranui*, which follows the lunar rhythm of the tides, sailing thirteen times a year from Papeete with about fifty passengers and 1,500 tons of freight.

Before going aboard, I visited a Swede who lives on Tahiti. Bengt Danielsson sailed on the *Kon Tiki* with Thor Heyerdahl and four other Norwegians in 1947. They had re-created an Inca ship—a great raft of balsa logs with sails and centreboards—and their idea was to see whether ancient South Americans could have populated Easter Island and other parts of the ocean.

Danielsson, past seventy now, has the beard, face, and skull of a porcelain Confucius, though his colouring is Nordic—a ruddy skin and eyes of grey flint shot with blue, like the ocean when the weather is about to change. I had to make friends with several fierce dogs before I could reach him in his library by the sea. He was surrounded by books on anthropology, history, and early travel: walls of books, piles of books on the floor, the air musky with old paper, buckram, and glue slowly dissolving in the humidity. He apologized for the dogs; they were necessary, he said, because Tahiti wasn't what it used to be. Europeans, especially French soldiers and bureaucrats, were apt to be roughed up by patriotic Polynesians. "Make sure you speak French very badly," he advised. "They seldom bother Anglo-Saxons or Scandinavians, as long as they can tell the difference."

Danielsson no longer subscribed to Heyerdahl's migration theories. While the Incas and their predecessors did visit parts of the Pacific, they did not populate the islands significantly. Genetic and linguistic evidence shows that the Polynesians came from Asia in a series of epic voyages by dugout catamaran. They first settled the Marquesas around the time of Christ, more than a thousand years after Tonga and Fiji—but centuries before they reached Hawaii, Tahiti, and New Zealand.

Danielsson loved the Marquesas. He had lived for a while in the Taipi Valley on Nuku Hiva—Herman Melville's "Typee." This was the place I most wanted to go. I wanted to see the stone platforms and sculptures Melville had seen, and perhaps meet descendants of the courteous cannibals he had described. Danielsson sighed the sigh of a man who's been asked the same question too many times.

"The Taipi tribe died out. Like most of the Marquesans. The population collapsed from invasion and disease." He reckoned there had been perhaps 80,000 Marquesans before contact; by the early years of this century fewer than 2,000 survived. Today they are recovering, but the great death, accompanied by a missionary onslaught, all but erased their culture and their past.

"When I was in the Taipi Valley in 1951 only four or five families were living there," Danielsson said. "And two of them were French." He saw me out, past his dogs.

"If you get to Taipi, ask for someone called Falchetto."

Captain Theodore Oputu of the *Aranui* was a far cry from the maniacal bully with whom Melville sailed. Though born in Tahiti, he was half Marquesan. The other side of his family came from the Austral Islands to the south. Most of his crew were from the Marquesas, and they all seemed to share a keen interest in body-building; there was a stack of magazines called *Muscle* on the bridge. Oputu was stocky, fortyish, and a demon chess player. He lived in a quadrilingual world—Marquesan and Tahitian were the vernaculars on board; French, naturally enough, the *lingua franca.* But everything was labelled in German. For the first eighteen years of her life the *Aranui* had been the *Horst Bischoff,* plying the icy ports of the North Sea. Then, after a midlife crisis and a $7 million facelift, she forsook Germany for Tahiti with new French owners.

Janice and I were in one of the old cabins below the bridge. It had once held a German officer and there was still a pre-*Aranui* sticker on the door—a bloodshot Kaiser Wilhelm face exclaiming, "*Heut' is nicht mein Tag!*" which I took to mean "This isn't my day!" I saw his point that night, when we crossed some of the deepest water in the world, Janice was woefully seasick, and twice I was emptied from bunk to floor.

As if to calm one's expectations, the *Aranui* stops half-way at the Tuamotu atolls. It was on a reef among these that the *Kon Tiki* came to grief, and you can see why. An atoll is a low ring of sand enclosing a lagoon and supporting a tattered fringe of palms. There are no hills, no streams, no ponds, no escape from the ceaseless crash of waves and the scratching of the wind in the trees, like a Brazilian rhythm combo. On big atolls such as Rangiroa, the far side of the ring is below the horizon, so that all you see is a crescent of sand stretching to infinity. You can walk for ever and the landscape will never change. You grasp this in a few minutes and realize that what at first looks like paradise is in fact a trap, a beguiling panopticon watched by the remorseless eye of the sun. The real scenery lies below the water, in the coral reefs that have raised the whole formation on the pursed lips of a drowned volcano. I was glad I had my mask and fins.

Another rough night and we approached Ua Pou, the first and tallest of the Marquesas, which rises abruptly from the heaving ocean to more than 4,000 feet. Nothing prepares you for the sight. "Like a piece of the scenery of nightmares," Stevenson wrote in 1888, comparing the cluster of rock spires to the "pinnacles of some ornate and monstrous church." The same comparison occurred to me, and I knew exactly *which* church, though it was unbuilt in his day: Gaudí's art-nouveau Sagrada Familia in Barcelona. The spires of Ua Pou have the same Gothic loftiness, the same weird luxuriance and curious, twisted menace. Tufts of rainforest cling to each crag and buttress, roots and creepers dangle into chasms. Gaudí could not match this setting, nor could he arrange Ua Pou's theatrical clouds. The vapours are never still, showing sometimes the base, sometimes the shafts, and, if you wait, a glimpse of one jagged summit then another in an endless striptease that seldom reveals the entire outlandish beauty.

Captain Oputu warped the *Aranui* alongside a concrete jetty at the village of Hakahau. Pale tourists trod shakily down the gangway; brown children swarmed up the mooring ropes and dived into the bay. The Marquesan sailors, in shorts and bright T-shirts, were muscled like gladiators, their smooth skins a canvas for strange geometric tattoos resembling Maya hieroglyphs. In the old days, before the missionaries put a stop to it, all people of note—especially veteran warriors—were ornamented from head to foot, like Ray Bradbury's Illustrated Man. The slow, painful process, involving ink and a shark's tooth, took decades to complete. The pain was part of the prestige; little by little the whole canvas filled up, until not even the eyelids and genitals were spared. Nowadays the work is more restrained, but I saw a man on our boat who had one foot tattooed like a tartan sock, another a thigh, almost all a shoulder or a bicep, and a fine ukelele player whose neck was ringed by an ornate blue collar.

These men, grinning and joking with each other and the locals on shore, slung down load after load of products from a distant world: Maggi Minute Noodles; Prego Spaghetti Sauce; French cheeses; Carolina frying chicken (whole legs, breaded); Superior Soy Sauce; Hinano beer from Tahiti; crates of Cheese Twisties; bags of cement; a dozen drums of gasoline; and, oddest of all, Yamaha Weedeaters. In exchange, they loaded sacks of copra—dried, rancid-smelling coconut meat, raw material for soap and margarine.

The economics are this: France, the last colonial power in the Pacific apart from the United States, subsidizes copra to about ten times its world value, which enables the islanders to continue living on their islands while enjoying a Camembert cargo cult. But there is a price: dependency. More than four-fifths of their diet is imported. Local breadfruit and yams are neglected; fishing has become a hobby; domestic pigs, chickens, and goats have gone wild. The Marquesans need the Weedeaters to keep the jungle from their houses. The empire costs far more than it earns, but the French think it's worthwhile because they can keep their infamous nuclear test site at Mururoa atoll and, more important perhaps, their Gallic pride.

From Ua Pou it was a short hop to Nuku Hiva, where Melville's ship anchored in the summer of 1842. The island grew on the horizon, beneath a sombrero of cloud, and in late afternoon we reached Taiohae Bay, an ancient crater eaten away on the ocean side so that two curved headlands embrace the harbour like the claws of a crab. Taiohae village, capital of the archipelago, has one or two small places to eat and stay, a Catholic church, and a splendid row of flame trees leading to the post office. The people live in modern plywood bungalows, but on the waterfront stands a restored Marquesan building from the past—a platform of boulders and cut volcanic slabs supporting a neat house of wattle, pole, and thatch. In front are modern sculptures of gods and heroes, only half-remembered after Marquesan culture's brush with death a century ago. Customs such as tattooing and carving these *tikis* (stone or wooden totems) have been revived, but the traditions are severed from their roots. Modern artists must rely on photographs and drawings made by early ethnologists; hence the historical authenticity of the men's tattoos. In many other Pacific islands—Fiji, Samoa, or the Cooks, for example—the fabric of native culture is palpable and alive, absorbing modern influences and transforming them. But here it seemed a self-conscious thing, struggling to resist the pressure of France, relying on preserved fragments of the past.

The rot had already started when Melville arrived. French warships and missionaries had preceded him, and the port was descending into the usual colonial brew of puritanical missionaries, alcoholic sailors, and trigger-happy soldiers. "The French," wrote Melville caustically, "already prided themselves upon the beneficial effects of their jurisdiction [on] the natives.... To be sure, in one of their efforts at reform they had slaughtered about a hundred and fifty of them." Even so, the influence of Europe was still tenuous. Before the anchor had touched bottom, the island girls swam out, climbed aboard, and danced with "an abandoned voluptuousness ... which I dare not attempt to describe. Our ship was now wholly given up to every species of riot and debauchery."

While their shipmates were nursing hangovers and aching backs, Melville and his friend Toby carried out their bold escape. They walked briskly through the native village and clambered up the steep sides of the crater wall, intending to drop down into the next valley, which they had been told was inhabited by a friendly, semi-Christian tribe. On no account should they go further, they were warned, because the valley beyond was the home of the warlike Typees, who kept to the old ways and had a sharp appetite for human flesh.

The amusements offered by the *Aranui* were more decorous than those alluded to by Melville. Some passengers chose to go horseback riding in the hills; others went by taxi for a picnic. They would end up at the Taipi Valley in the afternoon. I wanted to spend the whole day there. My original plan was to scramble up the mountains as Melville had done, but one look at the terrain was enough to scotch that. Instead we hired Richard, a young Tahitian, to take us in his four-wheel-drive Toyota. We set off up a steep dirt road that soon gave views of Taiohae's great green amphitheatre and grasping headlands. Reggae pulsed from Richard's tape deck, banishing the world of *Typee.* But Melville returned when we reached the high plateau that forms the core of the island. Janice and I sat on the edge of a bluff, munched our sandwiches, and tried to trace his route.

He and Toby failed, of course, to reach the friendly valley next to Taiohae. They had wandered for days from ridge to ridge, and slithered down a precipice draped in vines and waterfalls that dumped them in the upper reaches of the cannibal stronghold. Our road crossed the same tableland and then fell in hairpins to Taipivai, the valley's only settlement. Twenty or thirty small bungalows were scattered below us among groves of breadfruit, coconut, and mango beside the rocky stream that gives the village its name. (Taipivai is Marquesan for Taipi River.)

Richard had never heard of Herman Melville, and he seemed uncertain whether he could help me find the things the writer had described—stone paths and terraces, megalithic gods and temple platforms. For my part, I had no idea how much of Melville's tale might be fact or fiction. Even his publishers had doubts about its authenticity, though they knew a bestseller when they saw one. Literary historians have argued about it ever since. Far from being eaten by the Typees, Melville was—according to Melville—welcomed into a chief's house and treated as an honoured, though captive, guest. It wasn't long before he fell in love with the old man's adolescent daughter, the bewitching Fayaway, whose "pliant figure was the very perfection of female grace and beauty" and who wore little but the "summer garb of Eden".

"Bathing in company with troops of girls formed one of my chief amusements," Melville admitted, giving his Victorian reader a thrill. He went further. He said he took Fayaway boating on a lake upriver, and one day she stood in the canoe, unwrapped her skirt (a skimpy piece of tapa cloth that she sometimes draped around her waist), and held it up for a sail. "We American sailors pride ourselves upon our straight clean spars," he added, "but a prettier little mast than Fayaway ... was never shipped aboard of any craft."

Richard didn't know the valley well, but he found someone who did—a white man, past sixty but vigorous, wearing shorts, a plain cotton T-shirt, and a blue peaked cap that said NO SWEAT. At first I took him for the local padre—he had a plump figure and that combination of smugness and mystique that priests often have—but he turned out to be none other than Jean-Baptiste Falchetto, the man Bengt Danielsson had recommended. Jean-Baptiste had been ten years old when the family emigrated from Nice in 1936, hoping that the climate would cure his father's lungs, gassed in the Great War. He had grown up in Taipivai and married a Marquesan woman. He had forgotten how to read and write, but he knew the Taipi country like a favourite book. We piled into Richard's truck and headed up the valley, thick with jungle and largely uninhabited.

One of the ancient temples had been cleared of bush, revealing several stone platforms flanked by standing figures about life-size but squat and pot-bellied, with their knees flexed and grim expressions on their faces, as if straining to evacuate their bowels. Perhaps they were: a diet of human flesh is notoriously constipating.

The higher we went, the more the tall green cliffs drew in, until the valley ended, as Melville had said, in a deep cul-de-sac with two slender waterfalls streaming like tresses of white hair from the canyon rim. Falchetto pointed to an older road whose course could be glimpsed beside the river, beneath a tangle of wild guava and palms along the bank. He offered to lead me back along it; he could show me, he said, a stone ruin known as the "Paepae de Melville". *Paepae* is the Marquesan word for the megalithic platforms on which the houses and temples of the old days stood.

As we tried to keep up with the barefoot and surprisingly agile Falchetto, ducking through undergrowth and scrambling over roots, I saw that this was no wilderness we were exploring. The overgrown road under our feet was ancient and well built—a stone causeway linking an endless succession of *paepae* stepping down the valley in terraces. The Taipi River had once flowed through a continuous garden city, home to a miniature civilization whose citizens numbered in the thousands.

This was the Typee that Melville had seen.

Whether we saw the very *paepae* on which the writer lived and loved, I cannot say. The bush was thick and dark, the ruins looked much alike, and Falchetto could no longer remember precisely which one tradition assigned to the literary Yankee. It didn't matter. The main thing was to find that the thriving and elaborate culture Melville had described was real. He had glimpsed Marquesan life in its final days, the last flowering before it fell to smallpox, alcohol, venereal disease, and an orgy of cannibal vendettas. Later comers—notably Paul Gauguin, who spread his own share of syphilis among the pubescent girls he lured from a mission school—saw only the wreckage wrought by "civilization".

But on one point Melville lied. Nowhere at all does the Taipi River widen into a lake. It is far too steep and narrow. The boating afternoons with Fayaway were a delicious fantasy.

EIGHTEEN

Walking Home

Twenty-three years have gone by since I left England aboard the *Tampico.* I've been back many times, to visit, not to linger. My parents still live there—not on the bleak North Sea but inland, in rural East Anglia—and we have long buried the hatchets from my youth.

I can't easily say where home is and what nationality I consider myself to be. One Christmas in London, about half-way through those twenty-three years, I suddenly understood that I could no longer pass for a native. I was buying a leather wallet for a gift, and the saleswoman said, "How big is your money?" It was a pricy shop and I thought at first that this was an odd version of the car dealer's old ploy, "How much have you got to spend?" But she meant it literally: what size were the banknotes of my foreign land? She wouldn't believe I was English. My dialect had changed; and the British, more than anyone, define people by the way they speak.

It happened again in Edinburgh. I went into a pub and ordered half a pint of "heavy". I made sure the *a* in half was long. At least in Scotland, I thought, I could still be taken for a Sassenach. Slumped on a stool beside where I stood at the bar was a Scotsman, a tuft of hair protruding like steel wool from his tweed overcoat. From time to time he muttered, as if deep in conversation with his beer mat. He had evidently been there a long time, smouldering with an obscure resentment. I tried to avoid contact. But when he heard my voice, the Scotsman cocked his head and stared up at me with pure menace, like a wolf disturbed at its kill. "From Germany, are ye?" was all he said.

I can seldom pass for a local in North America either. People say, "You're English or Australian, aren't you? I can tell by your accent." (They have neither the ear nor the terseness of the British.) I've had to face it: I've become as mid-Atlantic as the DJs on those pirate radio ships that floated off the shore of my youth. Anthropologists call this "acculturation", though my case is very mild compared to those I've written about. To change voluntarily, if passively, from English to Canadian is nothing at all beside the *castellanización* forced on the Maya, or the deaths of entire languages.

Mine is less a loss than an embarrassment of riches. I have two homes: one English, parental, and ancestral; the other a wooded corner of Ontario where Janice (who is a real Canadian) and I have begun to put down roots. But anyone who has ever had two homes will know that something important is always at the place where one is not.

I'm a southerner, so the Peak District, near Manchester, had never been home in any personal way. I hadn't visited this part of England since my Cambridge years, when I'd done some hiking in the hills. But it gave me a strong sense of return—perhaps *because* there had been no visits over the years, no gradual drift apart. Here in the north, far from the trendy seventies and the Thatcher binge of the eighties, there seemed to linger more of the England I remembered, the England I left when I sailed to Mexico with Captain Sánchez.

THEY SAY YOU can always tell an Englishman but you can't tell him much. One way to spot him is to see if he stares at the ground when he walks. It's an unbecoming habit I've been trying to shake ever since I left the old country twenty years ago. I'd forgotten why I did it, but during my first few minutes in Matlock Bath I was reminded of the reason. Dogs. Something soft and yielding underfoot, rather like the pile on a good Persian rug, only it doesn't spring back and it's more likely to be the pile of an Afghan hound.

I'd been striding briskly along one of the nature trails, looking up at the dramatic limestone cliffs above the river, and hoping to find a warm pub before rain fell out of the oyster sky. The wind was cold and sharp with the sulphurous tang of coal fires. The Peak District is rich in industrial relics—Richard Arkwright's first cotton mill, founded in 1771, is just down the road from here, and on a hill above it stands the Middleton Top Engine, one of the oldest working steam devices in the world, an affair of rivets and beams built in 1829 to haul ore trains up the slope by cable. Mills, mines, and lead smelters are silent now, but I could still smell the foul breath of the Industrial Revolution exhaled by a hundred living-room chimneys.

The rain kept its promise; I slithered back down the trail, passed a Victorian bandstand, and crossed the Derwent by a cast-iron bridge erected in honour of Queen Victoria's 1887 jubilee. Matlock Bath had once been fashionable, the sort of place where the Victorian new rich—mill owners and upper management—came "to take the waters". Now it had a trampled, worn-out look. A theme park called, of all things, the Heights of Abraham, crowned rows of grey stone houses stepping up a hillside (they say that one of Wolfe's officers thought it looked like Quebec).

What sort of people come here nowadays? It wasn't an easy question. At the place I was staying I'd parked beside a bright pink Jaguar V12 which, on closer inspection, had seen its prime. A cinder cone of cigarette butts erupting from the ashtray threatened to engulf the white leather seats, and its owner was not a *soignée* woman with matching shoes and nailpolish, as I'd imagined, but a hard-looking character with a denim jacket and a Hitler moustache. Then there were the busloads of little old ladies who looked like the granny in a Giles cartoon—hats covered in plastic cherries, umbrellas with goose-head handles. They rode up the Heights in the cable car and were connoisseurs of cream teas and gift shops selling wrinkly rubber dogs. Here and there in front gardens and alleyways you saw Harley Davidsons with ape-hanger handlebars and fringed saddles. The bikers spent rainy afternoons in an amusement arcade, where a sign said NO LOITERERS OR FISH AND CHIPS. What are amusement arcades for, if not for loitering?

The bikes took me back to 1966, the last time I'd visited the Peak District. You never saw a Harley in those days. It was the time of the Mods and Rockers. Mods had khaki anoraks and crewcuts, they took nasty little leapers called purple hearts and rode Italian scooters dripping with chrome. The Rockers wore black leather, sky-blue jeans, and white silk scarves; their drug of choice was literal speed: they favoured souped-up Triumphs, Nortons, and BSAs—anything capable of "doing the ton", which was quite an achievement on the British roads of the period, to say nothing of the bikes. I'd ridden over the frozen moors in midwinter on a 1938 Velocette 500, a machine with a single cylinder, uncertain lights, and no rear suspension. Today it would be a collector's item; then it cost me £15. I remembered how cold that journey was, how I arrived in Manchester with ice plastered to my body like a suit of armour. Matlock Bath reminded me of lots of things; most of all it made me think of why I'd left this country.

Such was the melancholy turn my thoughts had taken when I

discovered the Princess Victoria. Here, in a building two and a half centuries old, was the business end of a coal fire and a selection of real ales. I settled into a seat by the fire with a pint of Boddington's, then tried the Old Baily Strong Bitter, which lived up to its name. I lit a cigar and followed with the Marston's Pedigree. Ah, the nutty, hoppy taste of good British beer. When I returned to the bar for a single-malt scotch to settle the ale, I noticed a tap offering Labatt's.

"Who would want to drink that here?" I said.

"You'd be surprised. It's not the same as it is in Canada." Steve Adams, the barman, poured me a taste in a shot glass. He was right.

"Know Paris, Ontario?" he said. "That's where I grew up." His father, an engineer, had gone to Canada looking for a better life, but a slump in engineering sent the family back across the Atlantic in the seventies. "Dad's idea of coming back to England was to buy a tea-shop in Cambridge. But instead we ended up here with the pub." The Canada that Steve remembered was the Canada I had arrived in—the gas guzzlers, the Trudeaus, Bobby Orr. Steve, still lean in his black T-shirt, had been good at ice hockey.

"Used to play with a kid called Wayne Gretzky. I hear he did quite well. His dad used to coach us. Hockey was serious business with the Gretzkys. Six o'clock every morning Wayne was out there on the rink in the backyard." He pulled me another pint of Strong Bitter. "Never kept it up here, of course. Now I'm a potholer. I go down every week." He tried to convey his fascination with spelunking—descending into the labyrinth of limestone caverns and old mine workings beneath the Peak District, wriggling through cracks, swimming across black, nameless rivers, diving through subterranean pools whose level can change abruptly when it rains on the moors. It sounded to me like an abstruse circle of hell.

"It keeps me thin," he said.

There are strange things seen in desolate parts of northern England. Towers in the mist, stone circles dating from the Bronze Age, ghosts of course. But I was unprepared for the sight of 200 gnomes gathered on the street outside the local chippy. Perhaps the Strong Bitter was to blame, but the closer I got, the more solid the gnomes appeared to be, until it was obvious that they were, in fact, solid concrete.

A striking redhead with a milky complexion caught my eye. She at least was flesh and blood. "Like a gnome, sir?" she called seductively. Business was brisk. She was moving more lawn ornaments than fish and chips. Gnomes had been front-page news lately. One Eric had been abducted from his front garden. This in itself was not unusual (gnome-napping was rife in England), but after a month or two Eric's owner got an envelope with Spanish stamps. Inside was a photo of Eric on the beach at Benidorm, reclining in a deck chair with a bottle of bubbly and a female companion. "Having a lovely time, wish you were here," the gnome had scrawled tipsily. Weeks later came another card, from Torremolinos. And then one day the miniature tourist reappeared at his usual post beside the milk bottles. The same old Eric, except that he had a wonderful tan and a grin that no amount of scrubbing would remove.

"I read about that," the redhead said seriously. Outrage clouded her pretty face. "I get any number of folk wanting another gnome because they've had theirs pinched. They get very attached to them, you know."

I'd imagined that the name of the Peak District—a region of uplands about twenty miles by forty—had something to do with mountaintops, but that's not so. The Peaks were an Anglo-Saxon tribe, the Pecsaetan, who occupied the area after the Romans left. The highest parts of the district are a mere 2,000 feet or so. The southern part, called the White Peak, is limestone country, its bald heights cross-hatched with dry stone walls dividing sheep pastures. Remnants of ancient ash and sycamore forest linger in ravines known as "dales" and "cloughs", old Anglo-Saxon words for valley.

The White Peak is circled on the north and west by a great horseshoe of hard gritstone the colour of rusty iron. On this, the Dark Peak, there are few walls. If it was ever wooded, there's no trace of forest now. The soil is a great sponge of ancient peat covered in heather and bunchgrass, blasted by wind, sun, rain, and snow, and severely damaged by the first acid rains in the world—the fallout from Victorian smelters. The place names are wonderful: Mam Tor, Via Gellia, Glutton Grange, Sourbutts Farm, Godfreyhole, The Roaches, Scraptoft, Knockerdown—as if all the invaders to come this way had left their signatures on the landscape.

I fled from the gnomes of Matlock and headed north to Castleton, a picturesque stone village graced by a Norman castle and blighted by a vast cement works. "Where there's muck there's money," northerners say, and they tolerate the factory because it offers the only alternative to waiting on tables and selling rubber dogs. The Peak District itself is sparsely inhabited by local standards, but about half of England's population lives within sixty miles, in grim post-industrial cities—Sheffield, Derby, Stoke-on-Trent—whose names belong in any textbook on the coal age. Twenty million people visit the Peak District each year—the same number that visit *all* of Canada's national parks. What would twenty million Canadians have done here? Covered these hills with those suburban eyesores known as "cottages"? If a city of Toronto's size can spread bungalows and barbecues to every beauty spot within two hours' drive, what would we have made of this?

Fortunately, the Peak District National Park is guarded by rigorous planning laws (to which Castleton cement works is mysteriously immune). Most of the twenty million never stray far from a tea-shop or a bus, and the ones who do are a hardy breed of hikers kitted out in kneesocks, leggings, scarves, and whopping boots.

Down in the warm public bar of Ye Olde Nag's Head Hotel all this gear of theirs seemed a bit of an affectation. I sat with a pint of Guinness in hand and a finely detailed ordnance survey map spread out before me. Surely I could nip up to the top of Kinder Scout—the highest place in the Peak—and back down the Pennine Way in a morning comfortably. Why was the landlord insisting I take food, water, and compass? And what was all this bother about mountain rescue stations? How could someone who had hiked the Andes get lost on a crowded island where the mountains were barely 2,000 feet and you only had to walk in a straight line until you tripped over somebody's garden gnome?

I set off next morning from Edale up a narrow valley called Grindsbrook Clough. The sun was out, the wind had died; it was absolutely glorious, as the English say. At first the stream ran through shady groves and burbled beneath quaint stone bridges. One expected to see a Romantic poet contemplating the pastoral scene; Wordsworth perhaps, studying a little pond, or Coleridge gazing vacantly from opium eyes. "Civilization ends at Edale," a chap in the pub had claimed—hyperbolically, I'd thought. But when I crossed the last stile and left the walled fields behind, I began to see what he meant. Grindsbrook climbed a wild chasm, devoid of trees but littered with boulders and loose rocks. The feet of countless sheep and hikers had worn through the turf into the clay and sand beneath; in places, path and brook shared the same bed. After an hour or so, I reached the crest, where the stream boiled from the plateau in a series of small waterfalls.

As my head bobbed up to the level of the moor it was almost taken off by the wind—a cold, damp, vicious wind that broke into my leather jacket and stripped the warmth from my body like a thief. The path petered out in a scribble of sheep trails; obviously each hiker had to find his own way. And the moor was not the heather-clad meadow I'd imagined, but a giant peat bog, a confused mass of spongy hummocks and deep, eroded gullies filled with soft black ooze and sheep dung. I pulled out my map, which immediately fought me like a snared buzzard. After subduing it in the lee of a boulder, I plotted a compass bearing and set off for the far side. I understood now why 2,000 feet felt high—the latitude here is the same as Goose Bay, Labrador; the wind rushes in angrily from the North Atlantic and the Irish Sea. It was like sticking your head out of a car window on a freeway.

The first few minutes were exhilarating rather than tough, but soon Edale fell behind me and I lost all sense of where I was going. There were no landmarks on the moor, only the next hummock, the next bog, beneath a thin veil of driven grey that threatened to thicken into mist. There was nothing for it but to trudge along, clutching the compass, hoping neither rain nor cloud would descend.

After what seemed like hours, I made the far side and was rewarded by a view of the warm lands, the green fields and wooded dales a thousand feet below. I sat in the shelter of a rock to devour my lunch (thankful I'd taken the publican's advice) before going down by the Pennine Way, which returns to Edale in a flight of stone steps called Jacob's Ladder. The map showed my perch as Kinder Downfall. The young Kinder River, which I'd followed from its source in the bog, escapes the moor here by spilling over a precipice. At least it was trying to—the wind fought every drop, whipping it off the rim of the cliff and sending it far into the air, where it atomized and fell as rain, turning my Stilton sandwiches to mush.

An indoor excursion seemed a good idea. I've never liked visiting stately homes, probably because my parents dragged me round them when I was too young to appreciate Gainsboroughs and Adam fireplaces. I was always disappearing into rooms closed to the public in search of the rest of the stag. There were two possibilities near Rowsley, about three miles from Matlock Bath. Chatsworth, a neo-Classical mansion of the *Brideshead* type, seemed predictable—the usual rococo and ormolu and putti on the ceiling. I gave it a miss. But Haddon Hall was another matter. Begun in the Norman period and completed at the time of Shakespeare, it afterwards lay empty for 200 years, escaping the brutal renovation or outright demolition that destroyed many mediaeval and Tudor houses during the eighteenth and nineteenth centuries. Haddon's owners, the earls (later dukes) of Rutland, moved to one of their other seats, leaving the old hall to its own devices. Its massive crenellated walls and lead-clad roofs fought a lonely battle with the elements until the 1920s, when the ninth duke made Haddon's restoration his life's work. The result of this singular history is probably the finest mediaeval great house in the British Isles.

Russell Jackson, the head warden, and Mary Lloyd, one of the guides, were closing the place up for the year when I arrived. It has no heating and is just too cold to keep open through the winter.

"I tried scrubbing the flagstones in February once," said Jackson, a jovial figure in gamekeeper tweeds, "and the floor of the banqueting hall turned into a skating rink."

"Tell him about your ears," said Mary Lloyd. You could see by the way she spoke that she was in love with Haddon. So was he, no matter how much he griped about the cold.

"Frostbite," Russell said. "In June."

Today the place was cool but not freezing. There were no other visitors; I could relish the sensation of travelling in time. It was as if the Middle Ages had just ended—the people and their clutter spirited away—and nothing had happened since. It was easy to picture the superb banqueting hall, built about 1370, as it would have been during a feast: the floor covered in rushes, dogs, cats, bones, scraps, rodents—all manner of filth, not to mention the raucous crowd of guests, menials, and hangers-on—while a fire consumed whole trees in the stone hearth, casting a smoky glow on the oak-panelled minstrels' gallery and the high table where the lords and ladies ate coarsely and voluptuously beneath a tapestry bearing the Royal Arms of England. This last, woven in the 1460s and said to have been given to a lord of Haddon by Henry VIII, still hangs above the dais, its rich red and blue designs a vivid foil to the rustic planks at which the diners sat.

I saw fifteenth-century murals in the chapel, intricate Tudor ceilings, extraordinary Elizabethan glazing in mullioned windows. But the banqueting hall affected me most. It, more than anything, was a doorway to the past. I thought: when that tapestry was made, the Americas lay undisturbed and unsuspected beyond the horizons of Europe; Christopher Columbus was a boy, and Moctezuma of Mexico had not been born. I felt far removed from the gnomes outside the chip shop down the road. And for the first time since landing in England, I felt I had come home.

Author's Note

"The Captain's Santo", "Going to the Wall", and "Return to the Islands" have never before appeared in print. The other pieces have been previously published as follows, although I have changed some titles and done some rewriting for *Home and Away*:

"An Antique Land", "Anatolian Badlands", "Invading Grenada", "Outback", and "Sex, Lies, and Escape" appeared in *Destinations.* "An Antique Land" and "Outback" also appeared in *The Washington Post,* and "An Antique Land" was reprinted by *The Travel Review.* "A Jungle Michelangelo", "The Death-List People", "Peru Is Not a Novel", and "Beyond Words" were published in *Saturday Night.* "A Jungle Michelangelo" was also published in *Time Among the Maya* and is reprinted here by permission of Penguin Books Canada Limited. *Condor* was broadcast on CBC Radio, *Speaking Volumes* and *Aircraft,* and later printed in *Canadian Forum.* "The Lamanai Enigma" appeared in *Equinox,* "Crossroads" in *Soho Square III,* "Does Canada Want a Wounded Knee?" in *The Globe and Mail,* and "Kangaroo" in *The Great Canadian Anecdote Contest.* "Walking Home" was published in *En Route.*

Sources of Quotations

P. 28: from Clifford Geertz, *The Interpretation of Cultures* (New York: Basic Books, 1973).

P. 73: from Hernández Xahil et. al., *Memorial de Sololá, Anales de los Cakchiqueles*, translated from Maya into Spanish by Adrián Recinos (Guatemala: Editorial Piedra Santa, 1980). My English translation.

P. 80: from Alfredo Saavedra, "Declaración Jurada", *Exodus* (Toronto: Latin American Canadian Literature Editions, 1988). My English translation. Courtesy of Alfredo Saavedra.

P. 113: the full text of the first song can be found in José María Arguedas, ed., *Canciones y cuentos del pueblo quechua* (Lima: Editorial Huascarán, 1949). The full text of the second song can be found in Rodrigo Montoya, Luis Montoya, and Edwin Montoya, eds., *La Sangre de los Cerros: Urqukunapa Yawarnin* (Lima: Mosca Azul, 1987).

P. 139: from Phil Ochs's song "Santo Domingo", © 1965, 1968 by Barricade Music Co., New York.

P. 147: from the Mighty Sparrow's song "Lying Excuses". Copyright 1986/7 (COTT). Courtesy of Dr. Slinger Francisco, Litt.—a.k.a. the Mighty Sparrow.

P. 156: from Gertie Tom, *Èkeyi, Gyò Cho Chú, My Country: Big Salmon River* (Whitehorse: Yukon Native Language Centre, 1987). Courtesy of Yukon Native Language Centre.

P. 162: from Emile Petitot, *Dictionnaire de la Langue Dènè-Dindjiè* (Paris: Leroux, 1876).
P. 164: from the Dawson City Archives.

P. 168: from Angela Sidney, *Tagish Tlaagú, Tagish Stories* (Whitehorse: Council for Yukon Indians, 1982). Courtesy of Yukon Native Language Centre.

P. 169: song translation by Jeff Leer.

P. 174: from Angela Sidney, *Tagish Tlaagú, Tagish Stories* (Whitehorse: Council for Yukon Indians, 1982). Courtesy of Yukon Native Language Centre.